Affirmations for Writers

By Ivy Starlight

Published by Shoushockie Publishing House

ISBN 978-1-950700-99-8

Paperback Edition

Printed in the USA

Introduction

There's a science behind affirmations. It's a well established psychological theory that using positive affirmations helps program the mind to achieve the desired results and goals that are set.

By using affirmations regularly, you can create lasting, long term change and success for yourself. Reading and repeating affirmations as a form of meditation, is an effective tool to help focus your mind and motivate you.

By repeating the affirmations, you will reprogram your subconscious mind, putting it on auto-pilot mode, you will be able to write without hesitation.

The magic that many believe in and have achieved by using affirmations is that it helps you manifest your dreams and goals through positive thinking with the power of your subconscious mind.

Using these affirmations for writers, will help you take action, decrease stress, improve self-esteem and stop procrastinating.

They will help you overcome any insecurities about your ability to write and remove creative blocks that prevent you from writing consistently.

Meditation for Writers

Meditation is a great way to plan a writing project. By relaxing the mind and releasing stress, you can access your subconscious minds creative source to bring forth ideas more easily to your conscious mind. Meditation requires a dedicated space to rest and clear the mind. Affirmations can be used anytime and anywhere, even during meditation.

Guided Meditation:

Find a comfortable position to begin the meditation. Now breathe in deeply... and exhale. Positive uplifting energy flows through every breath that you take and replenishes your body. Inhale and feel your feet, calves and thighs relax. Slowly exhale. Again inhale deeply and feel your hips, buttocks, belly and lower back sink in and relax deeply. Then exhale and feel the release of any tension in your lower body. Feel the wonderful calm wash over you. Take in a long and deep breath, and feel your chest, back, shoulders, arms, and hands become deeply relaxed by your sides. Then exhale. Now, as you breathe in again, feel your neck, jaw, face, eyes, head and crown become completely relaxed and feel the tension releasing from your upper body completely. Breathe out a blissful sigh of relief.

Now, with your minds eye, envision a beautiful library. It is empty and reserved just for you to spend some time researching and writing your next masterpiece. The soaring ceilings and vast space give your spirit freedom to roam and explore.

You walk through aisles and browse through the categories of books. You find your favorite genre and then to your surprise you see a shelf that captures your attention. You notice that your name is printed on one of the books. You open the book and discover it's a title that you published, in the future! The date inside of the book clearly states a year that has yet to be! Then you notice the shelf is full of your publications.

You feel an otherworldly sense of confidence in yourself and this inspires you with a strong urge to write. With a smile and a spring in your step, you explore the rest of this beautiful, enchanting library. You realize that you are here because of your ability to write. You are a great writer.

Finally, you find the perfect spot to sit and write. In a grand hall of tables and chairs, you choose your seat and pull the chain on a table lamp. The light turns on in a warm and toasty glow over a blank notebook and pen that are ready for you to write with. In this perfect space, you begin writing.

Meanwhile, within yourself as the meditating watcher, your mind now plans what it wants to write about. There are several ideas flowing through you, however, the boldest idea captures your attention first.

Now, clear your mind and start to meditate upon that idea, only giving your full attention to it without any distractions. Focus your mind completely on this brilliant idea. Let this idea expand itself and take on a life of its own. Spend a few moments experiencing your multi-faceted idea. Pay attention to the thoughts, feelings, voices, and visions it reveals and produces.

Once you have a strong sense of the idea you wish to capture on paper, it is time to leave the library. Now, bring your awareness back to your current space. Take a few deep breaths, while holding onto your great idea, you are ready to get up and start writing.

You know that your perfectly planned idea will result in your success. Whenever you need to free yourself of a block, meditation will unlock your inner flow of thoughts and ideas immediately and you will be able to write without hesitation.

By entering a meditative state you can access your ideas through the power of creative visualization. Your mind is a creative goldmine that flows in harmony with the collective consciousness of all.

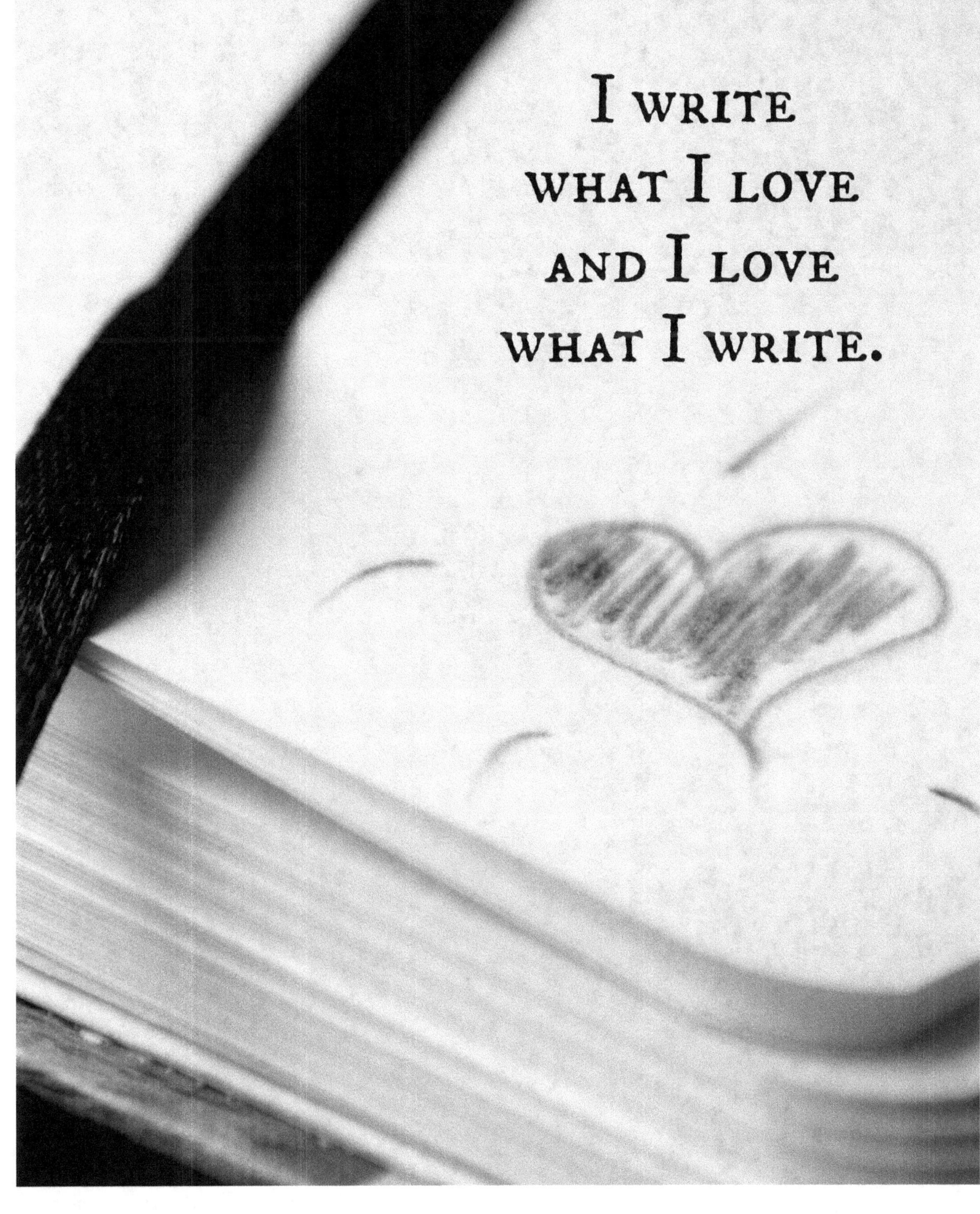

I write
what I love
and I love
what I write.

WRITING IS MY FAVORITE THING TO DO.

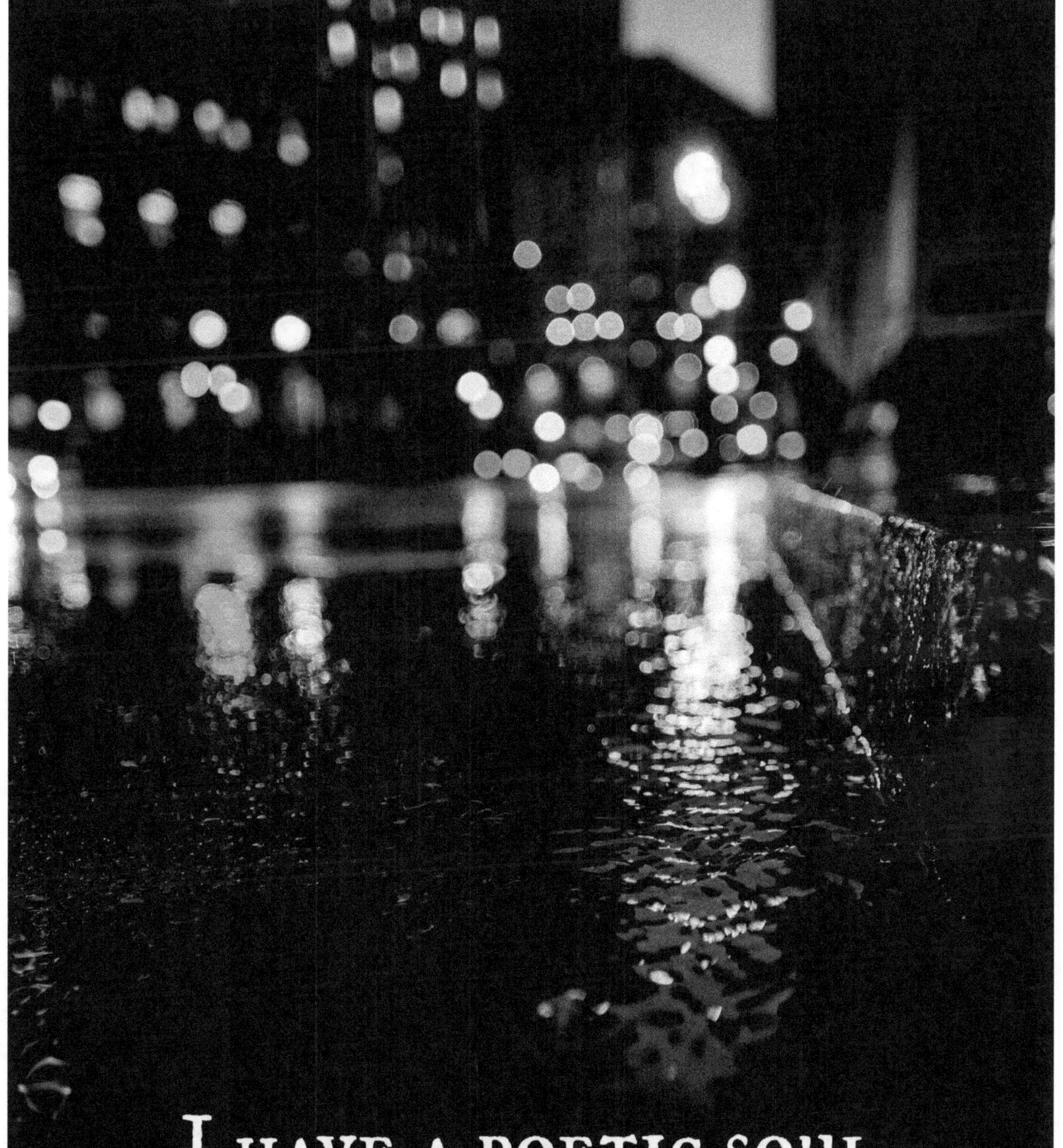
I HAVE A POETIC SOUL.

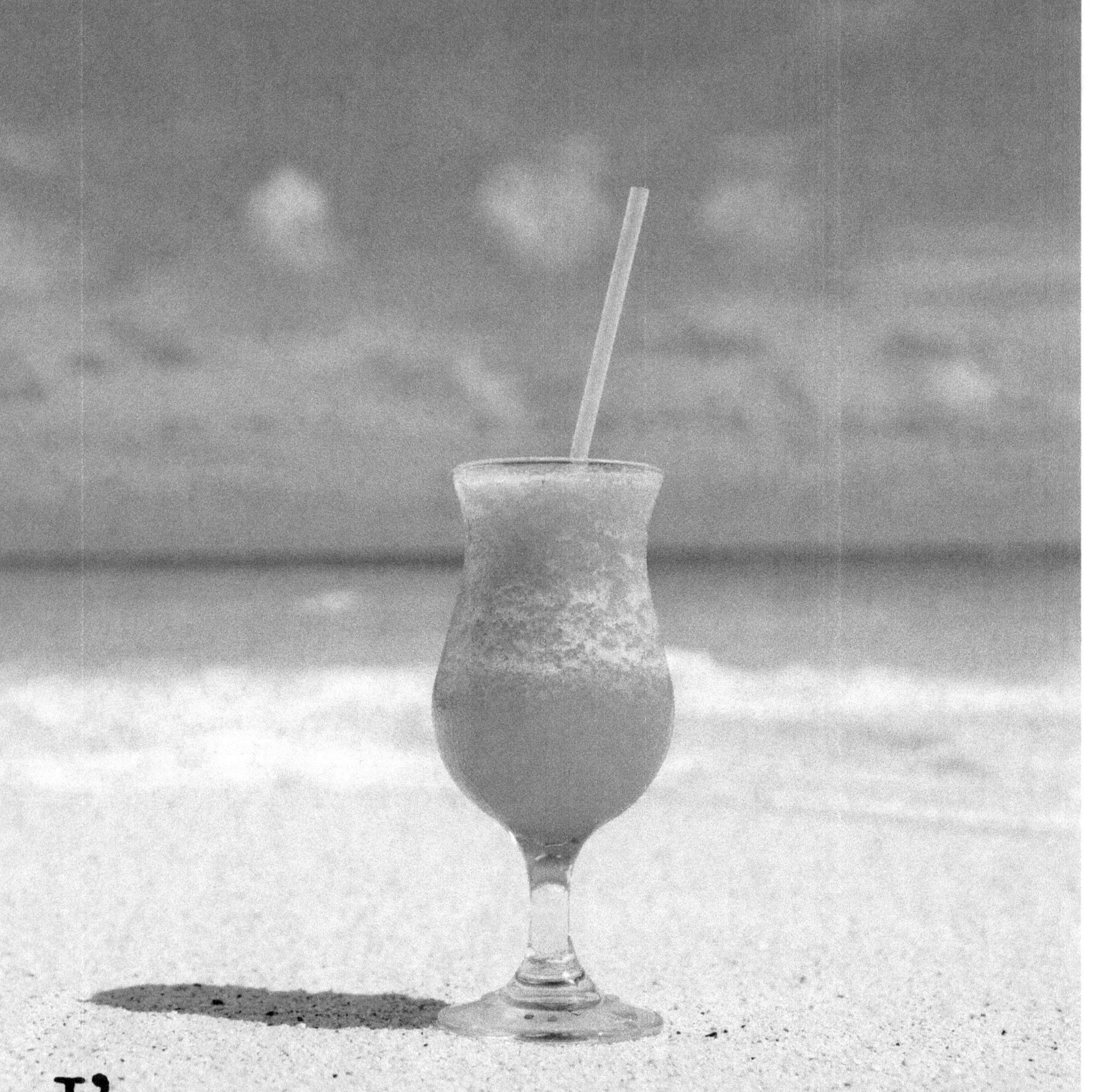

I'M ON VACATION EVERY DAY
AS A WRITER.

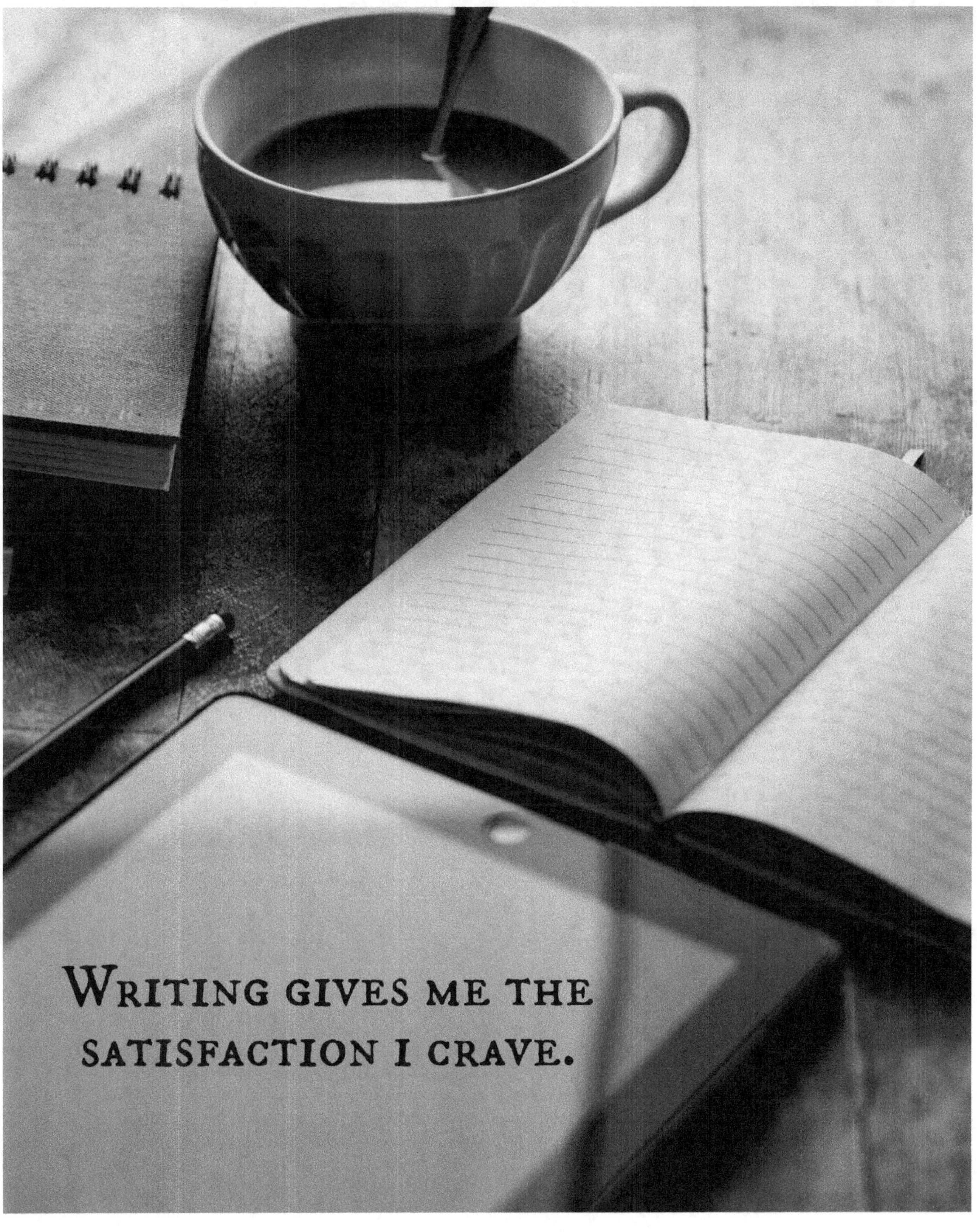

WRITING GIVES ME THE
SATISFACTION I CRAVE.

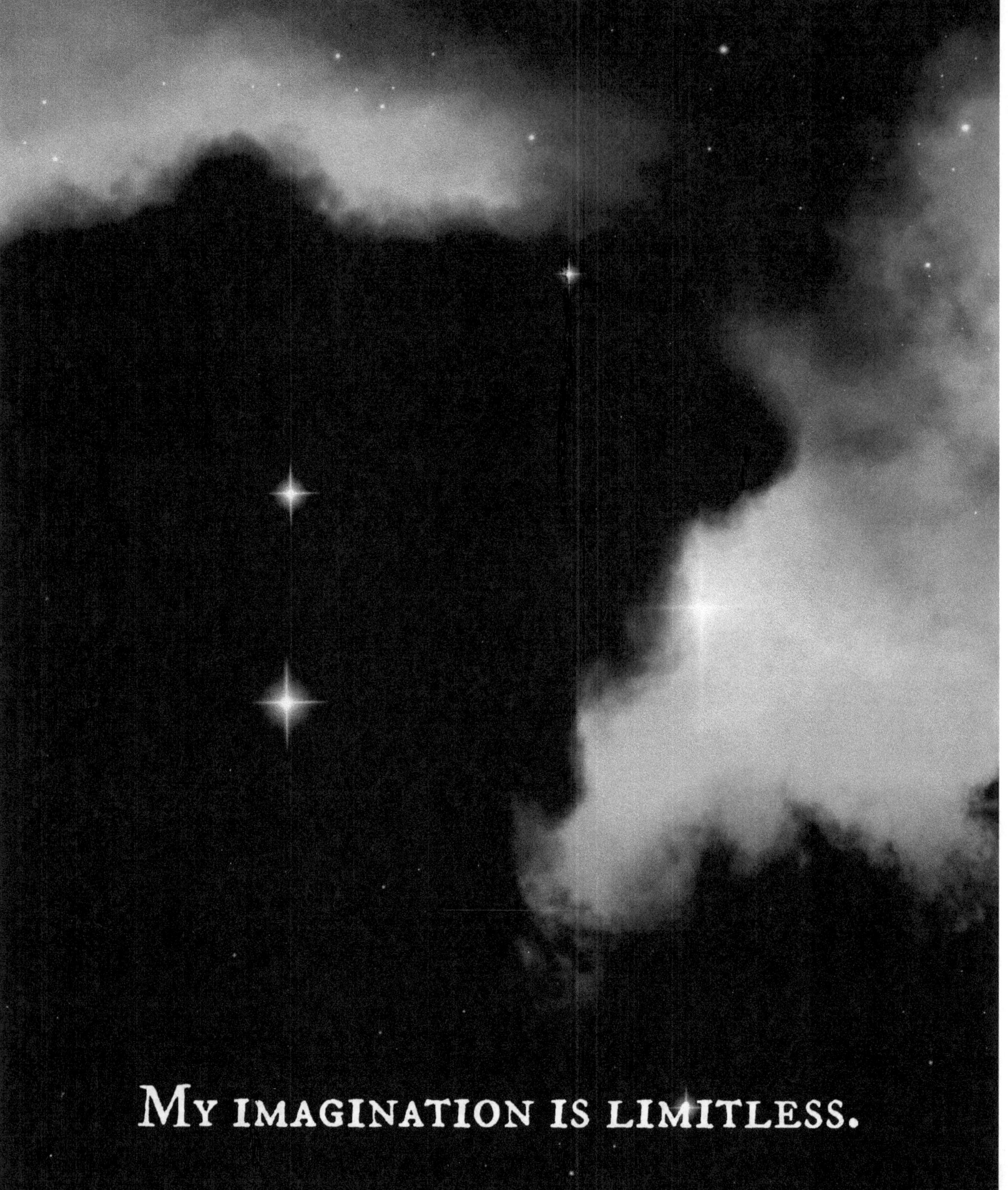
My imagination is limitless.

I FOLLOW MY BLISS BY WRITING CONSISTENTLY.

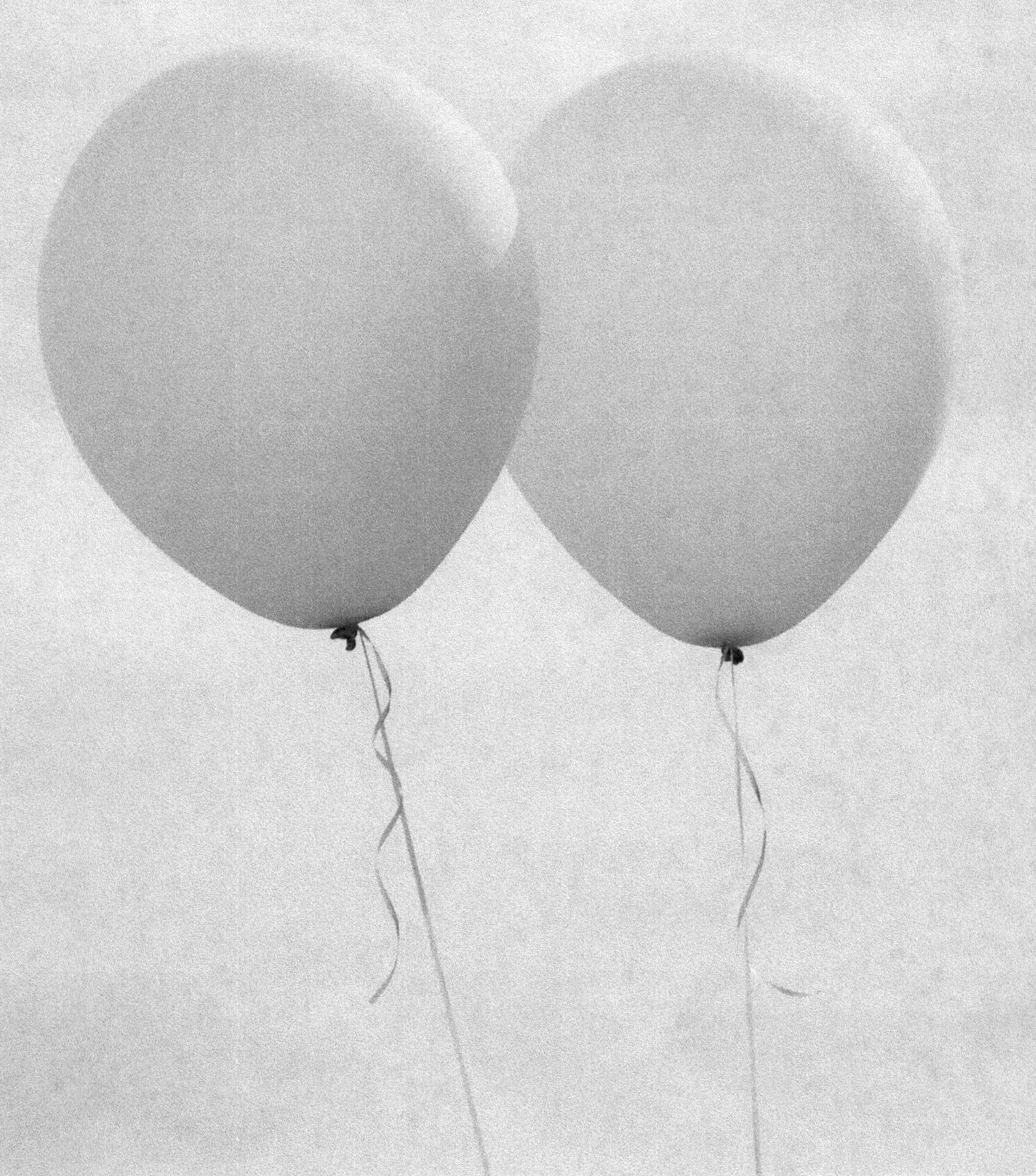

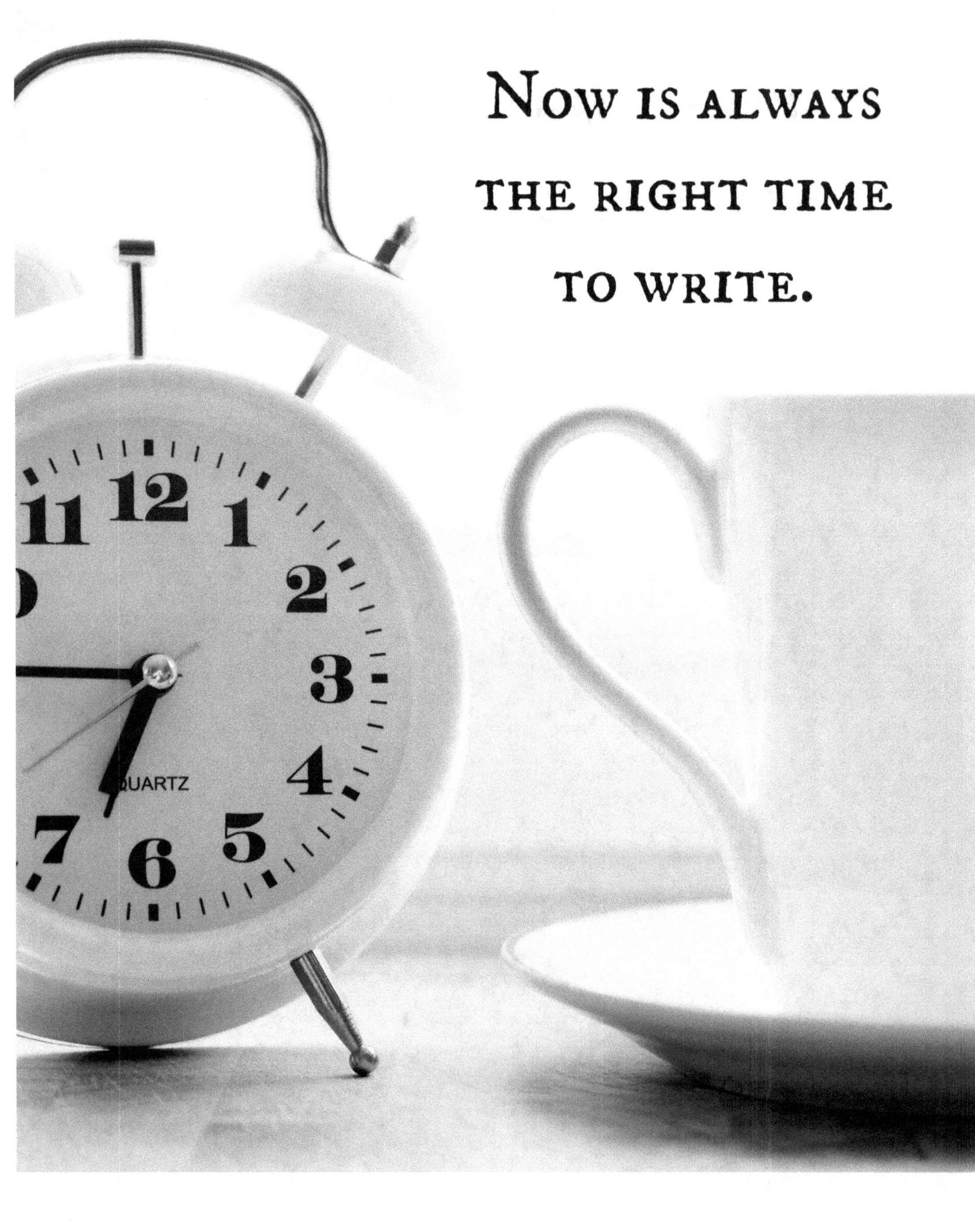

Now is always
the right time
to write.

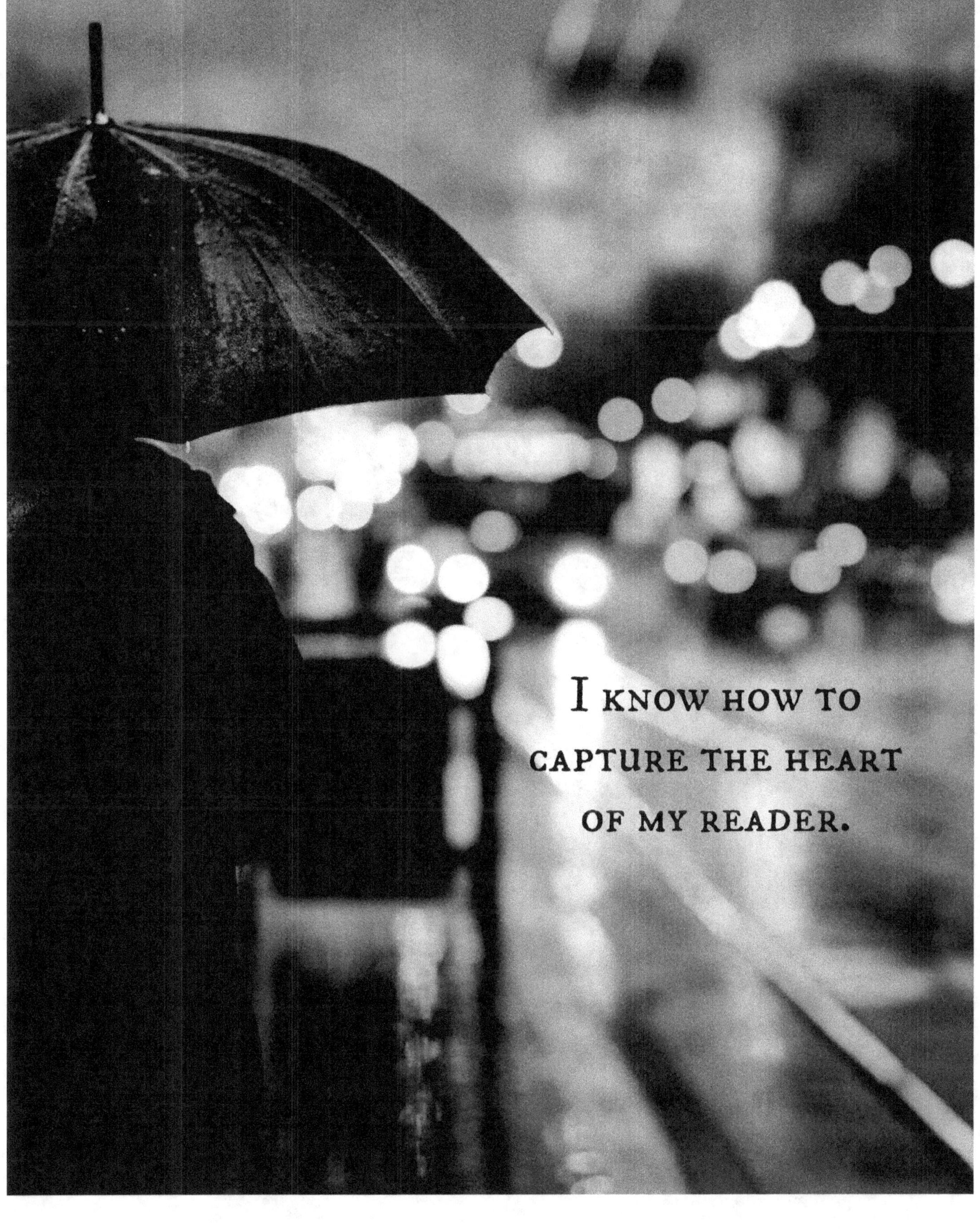
I know how to
capture the heart
of my reader.

THE GREATEST WISDOM
OF THE UNIVERSE
FLOWS THROUGH MY PEN.

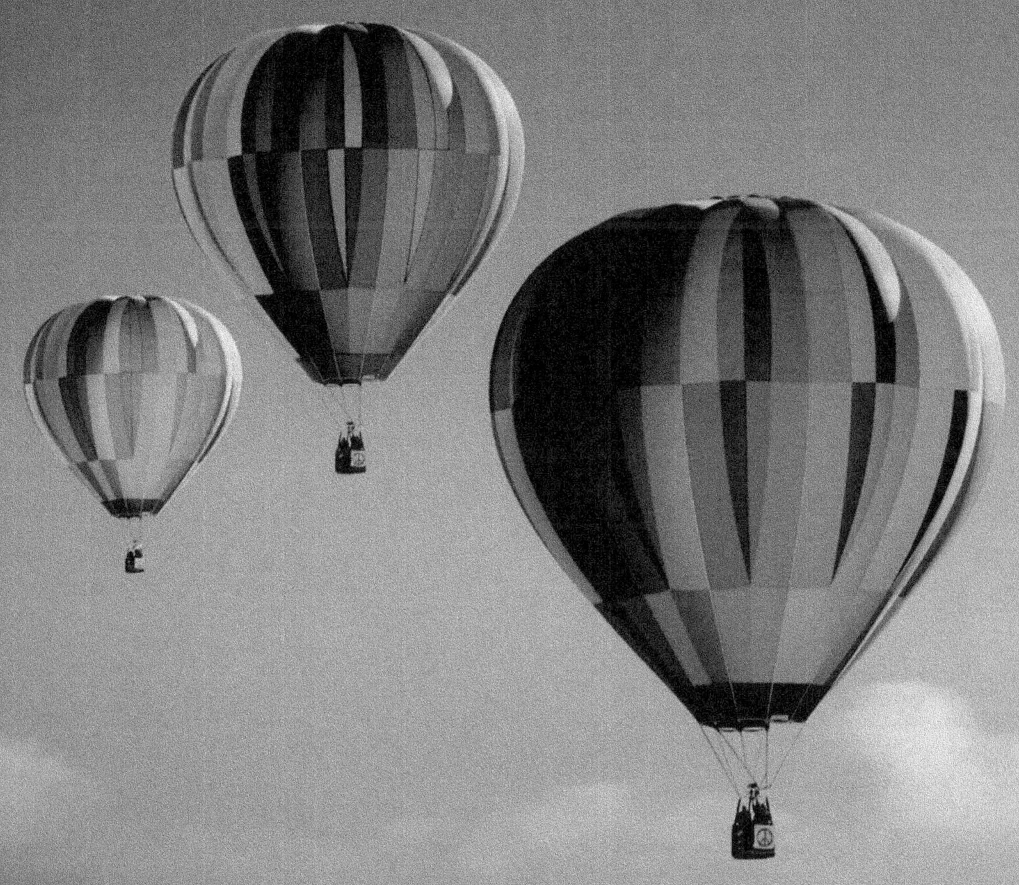
WRITING IS MY FUN TIME.

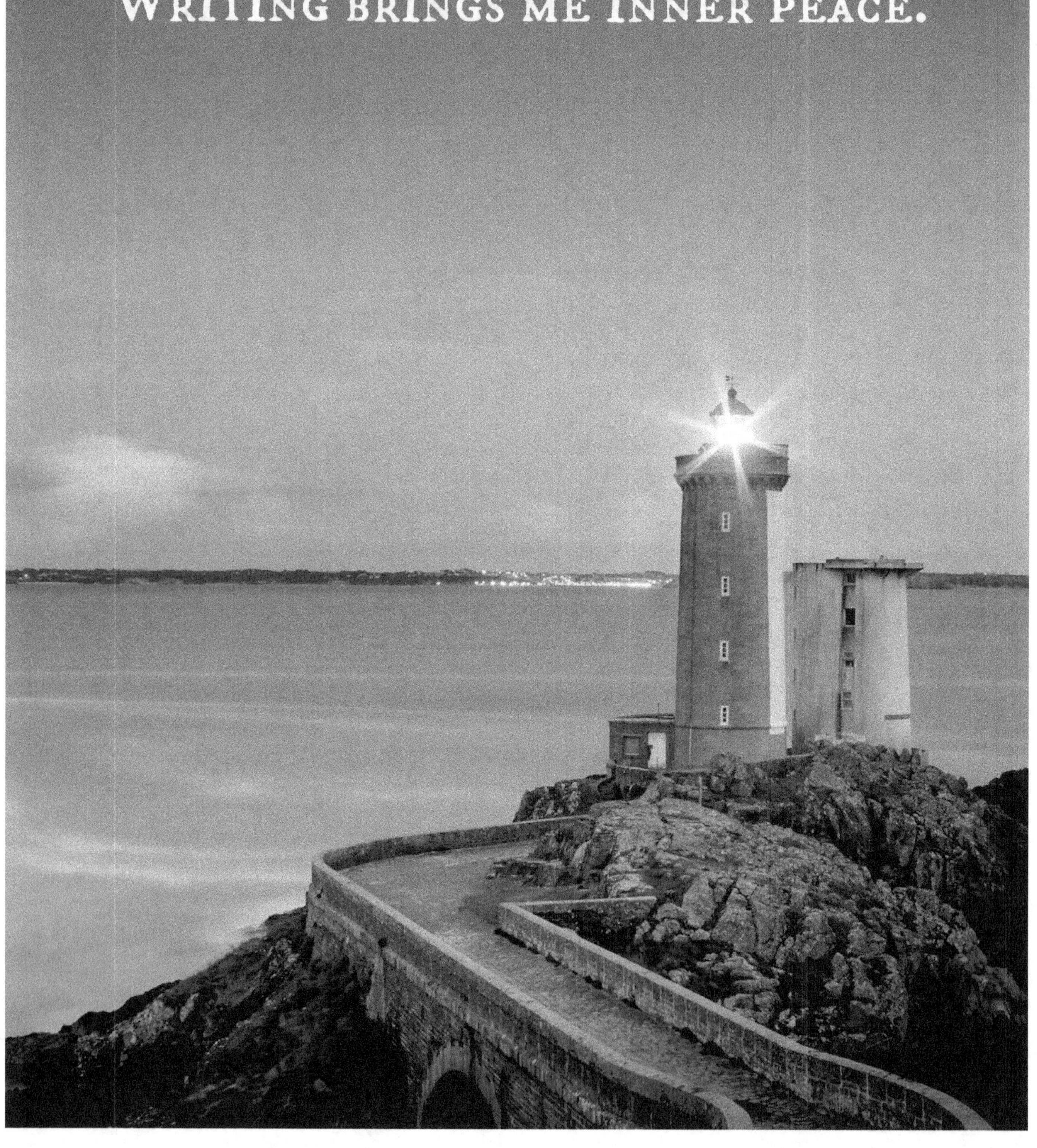
Writing brings me inner peace.

I am a talented author.

WRITING IS
MY GUILTY
PLEASURE.

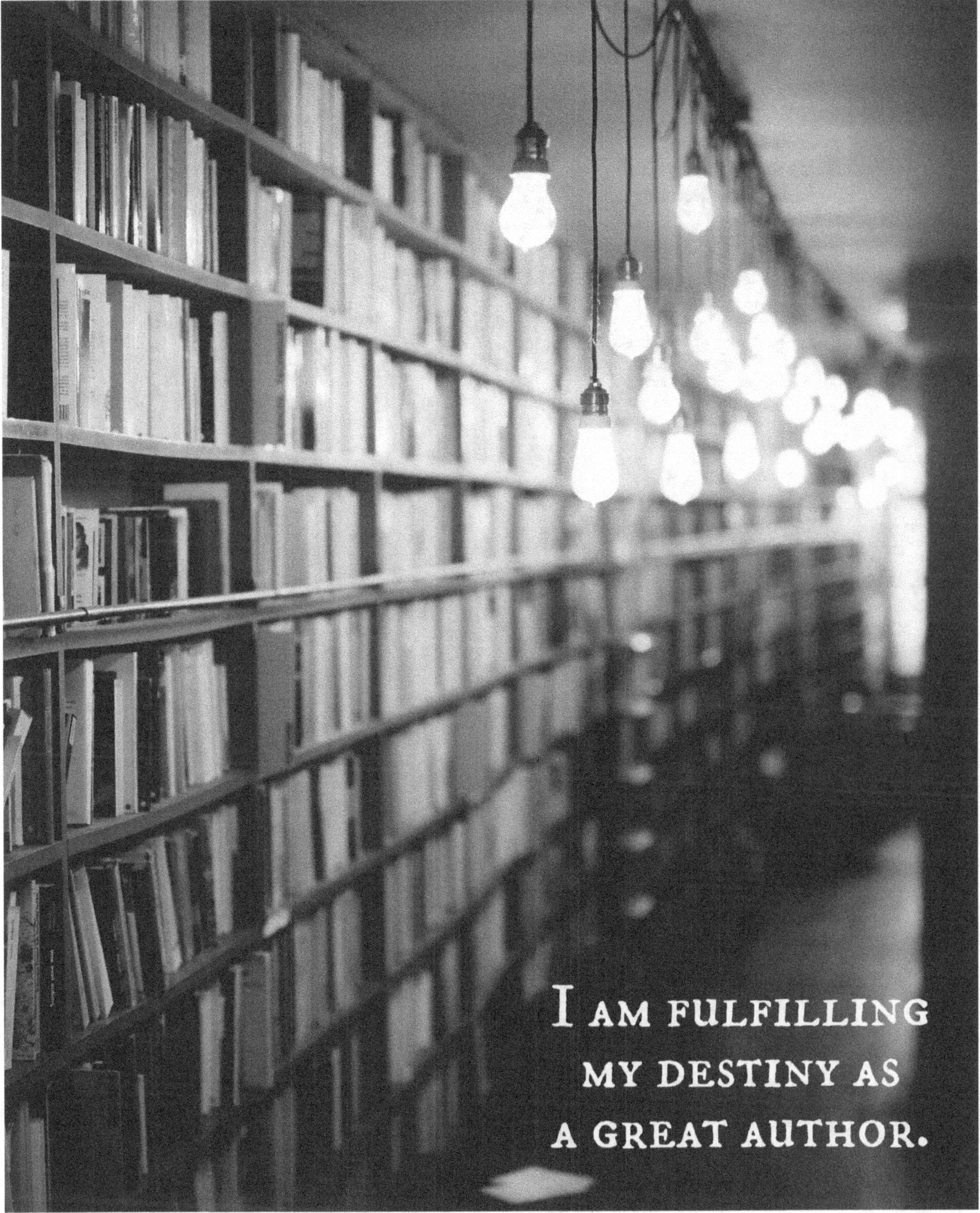
I AM FULFILLING
MY DESTINY AS
A GREAT AUTHOR.

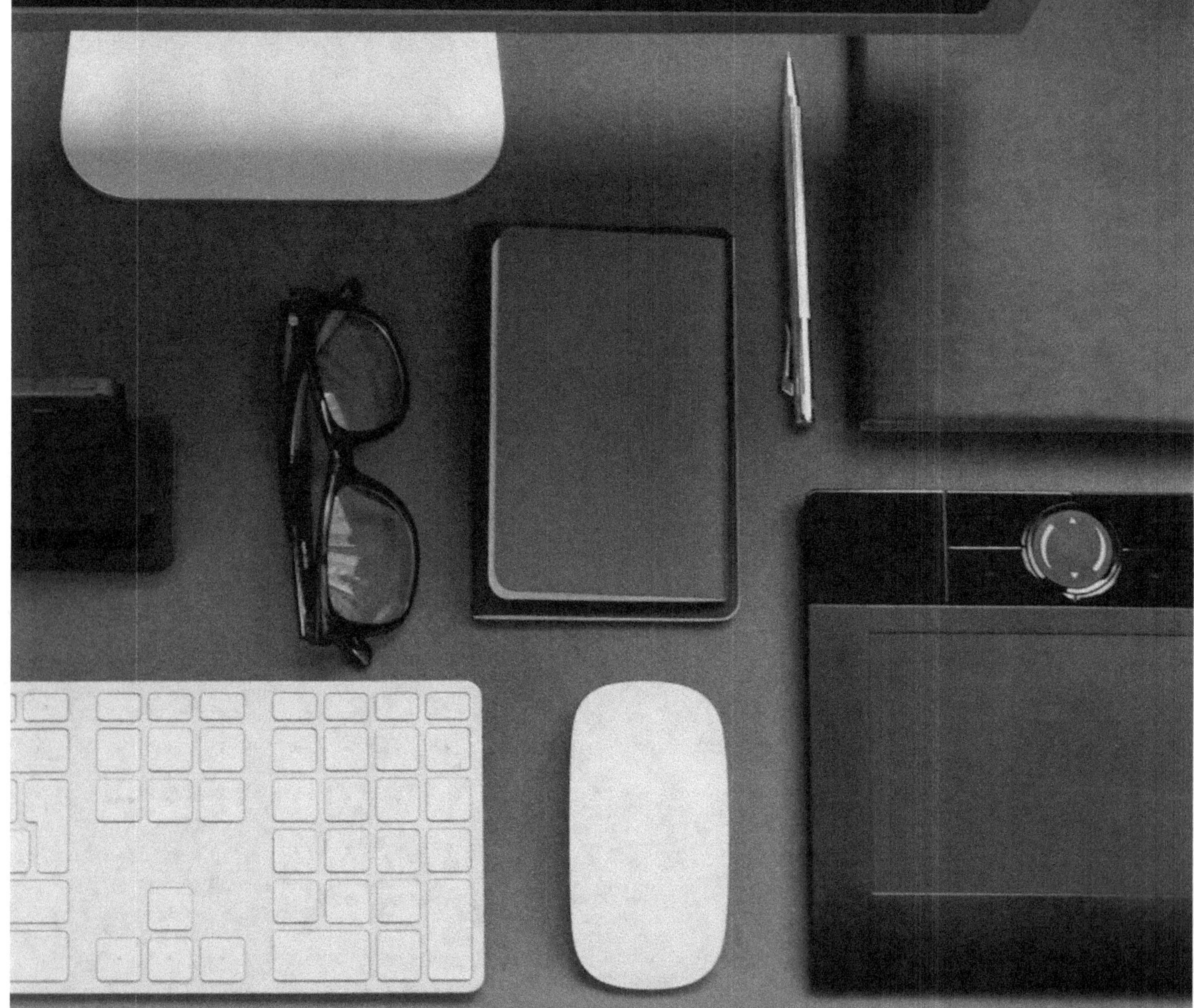
I always make time
to write every day.

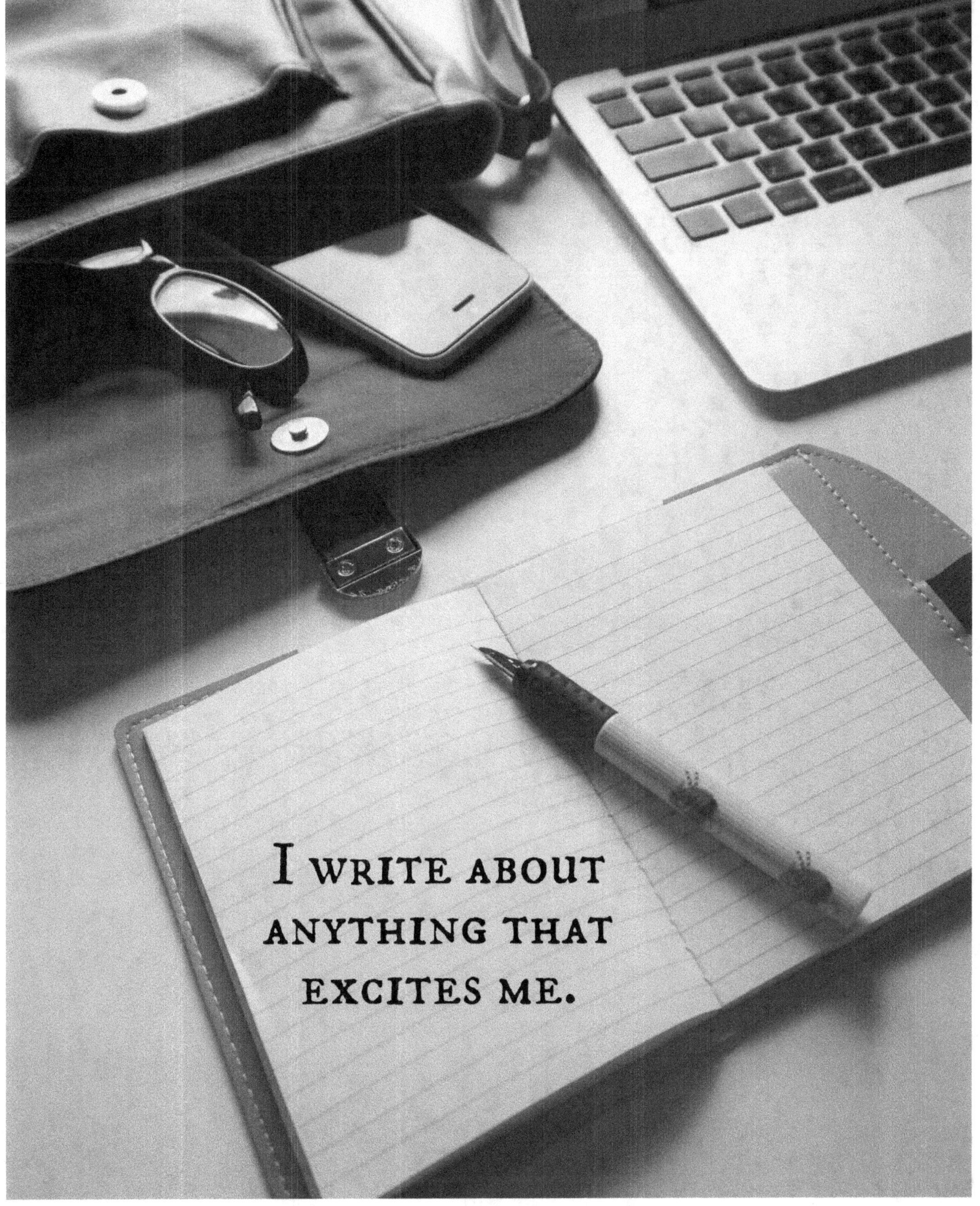
I WRITE ABOUT ANYTHING THAT EXCITES ME.

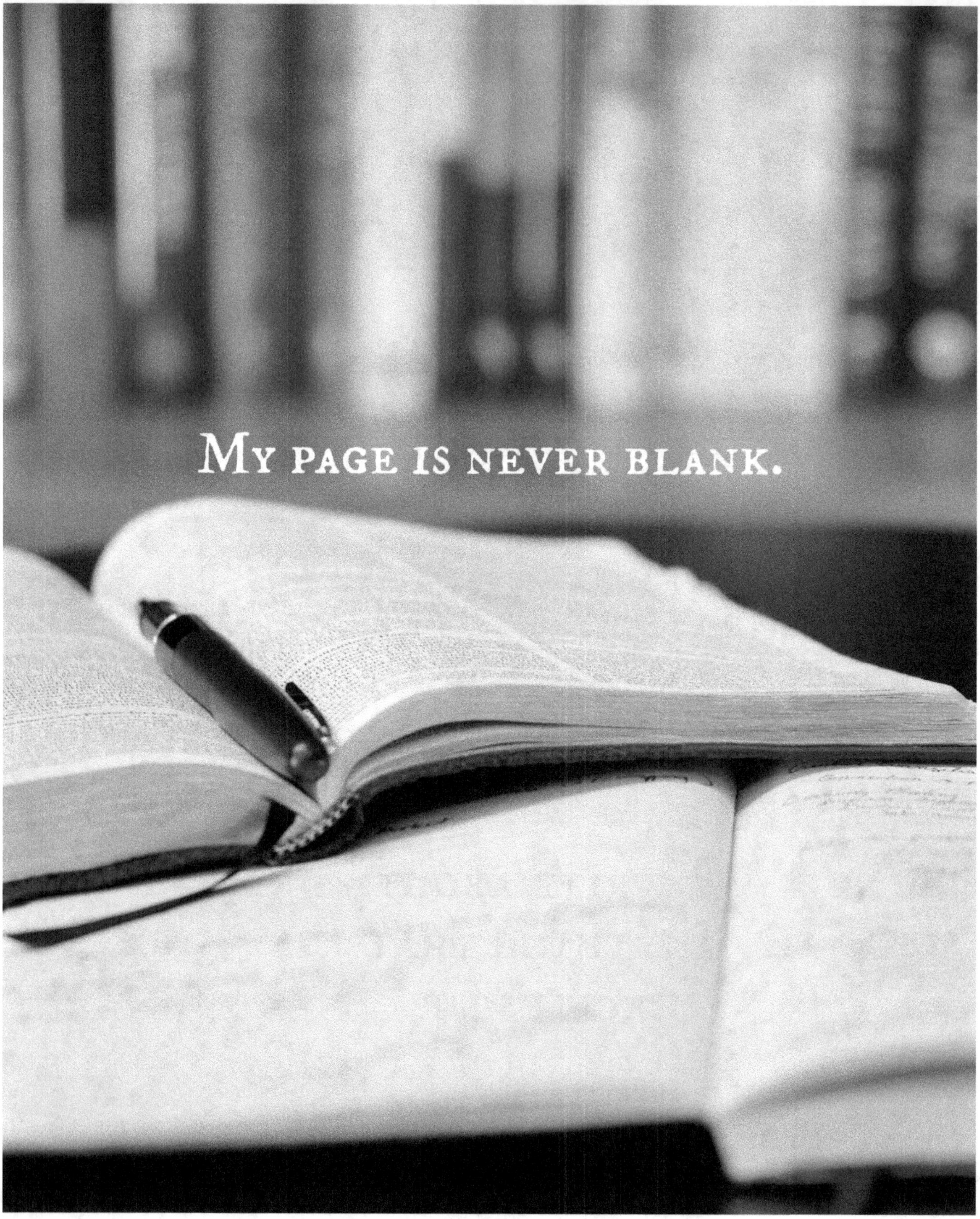

My page is never blank.

I love to write.

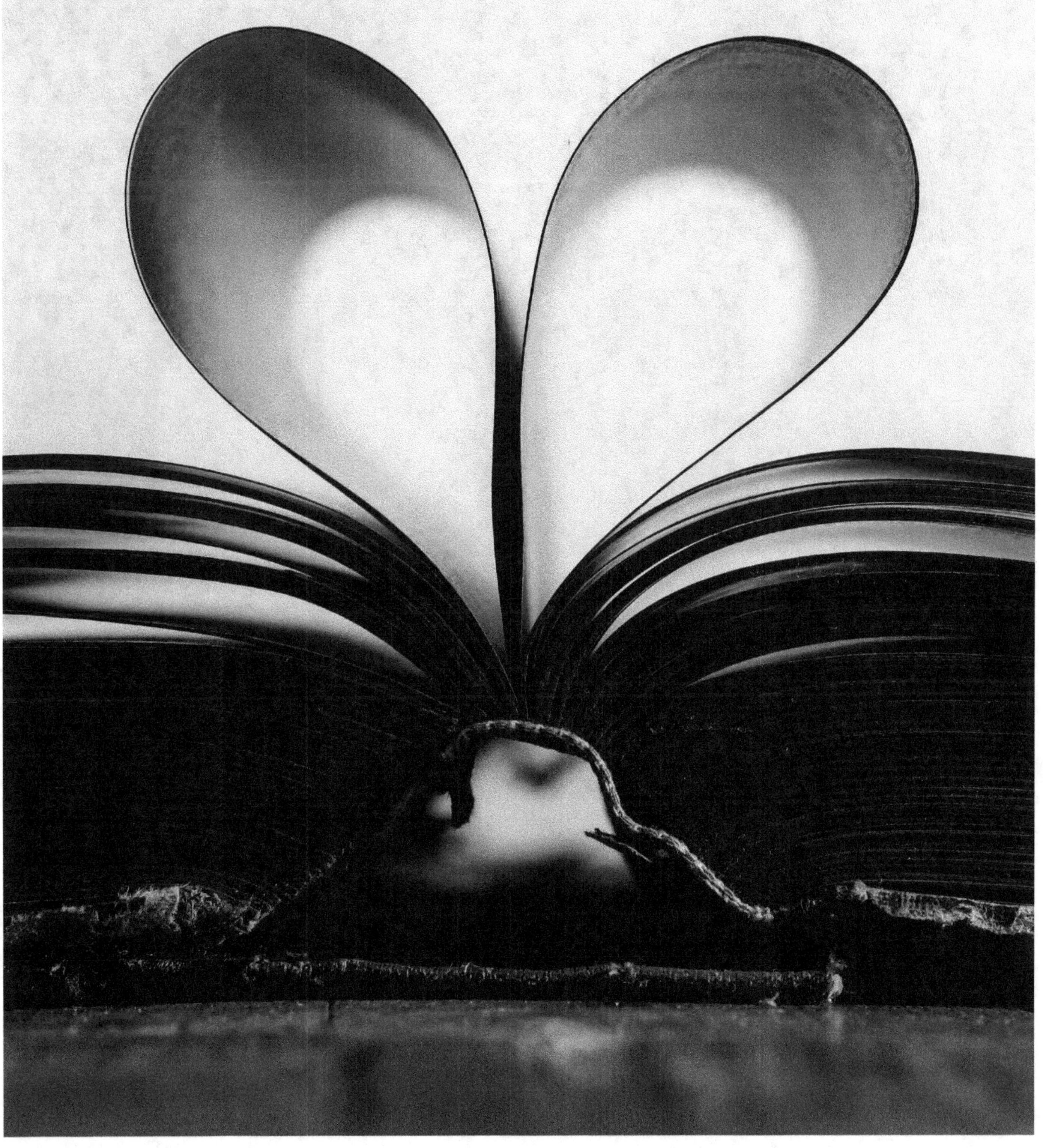

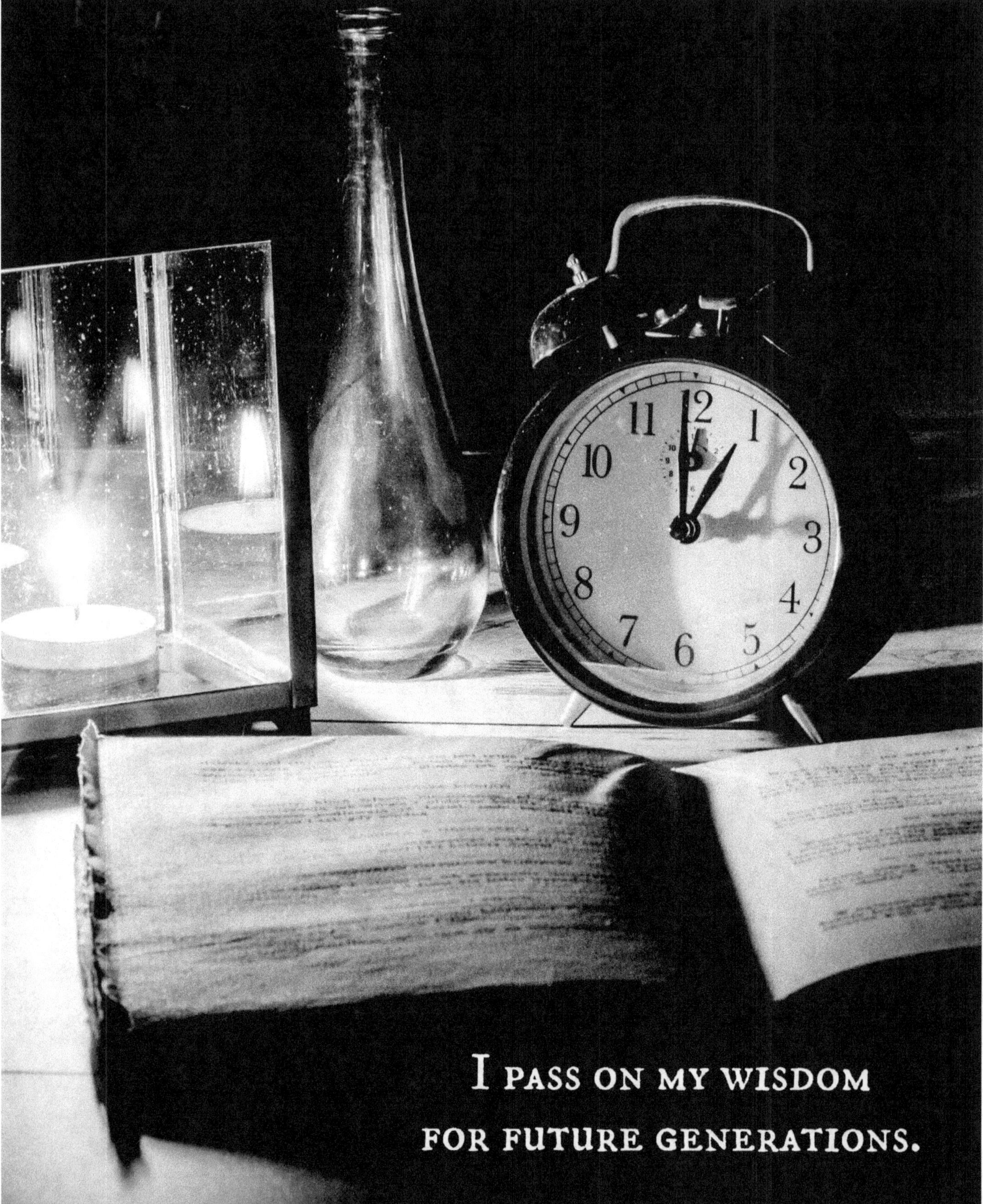
I PASS ON MY WISDOM
FOR FUTURE GENERATIONS.

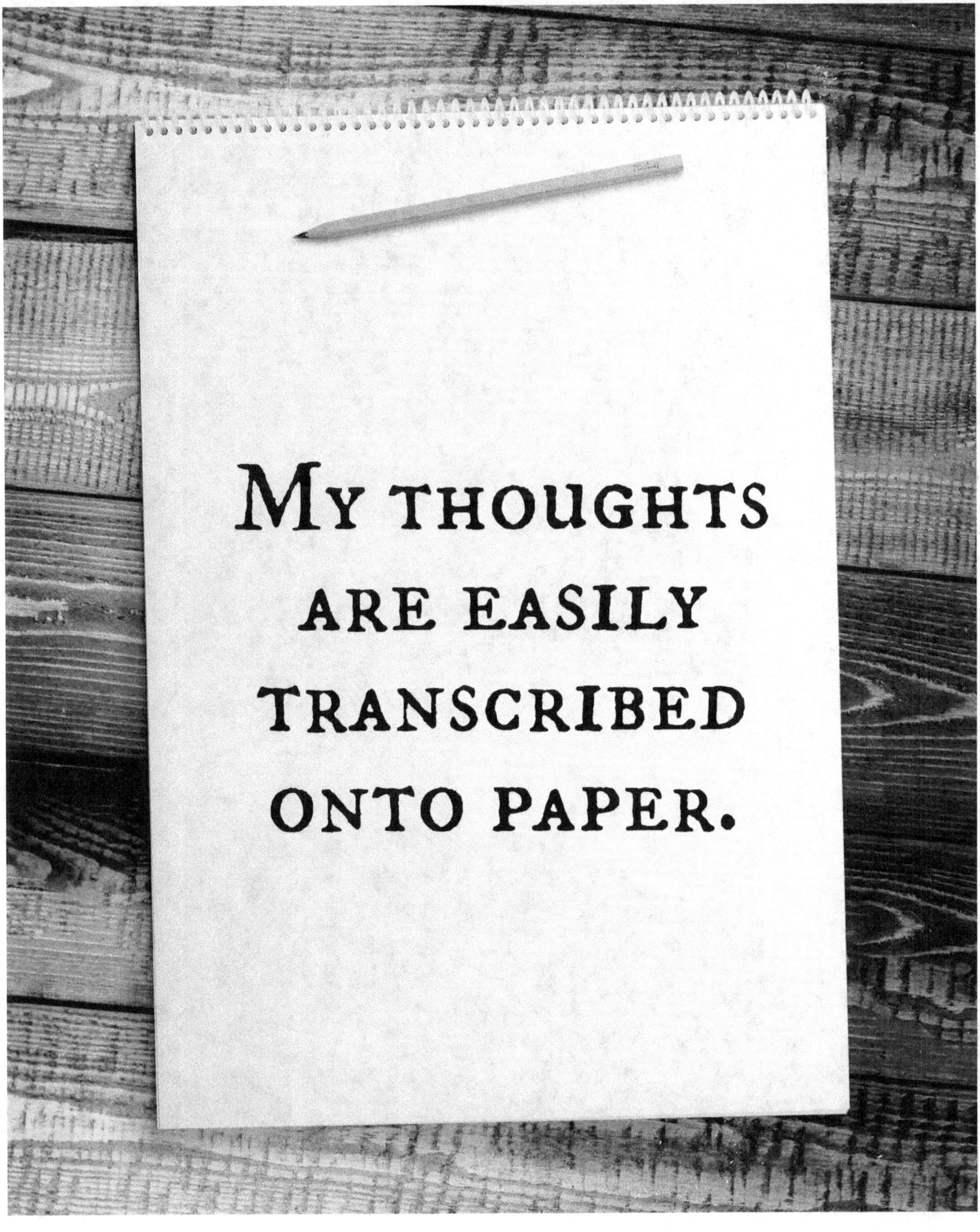

My thoughts
are easily
transcribed
onto paper.

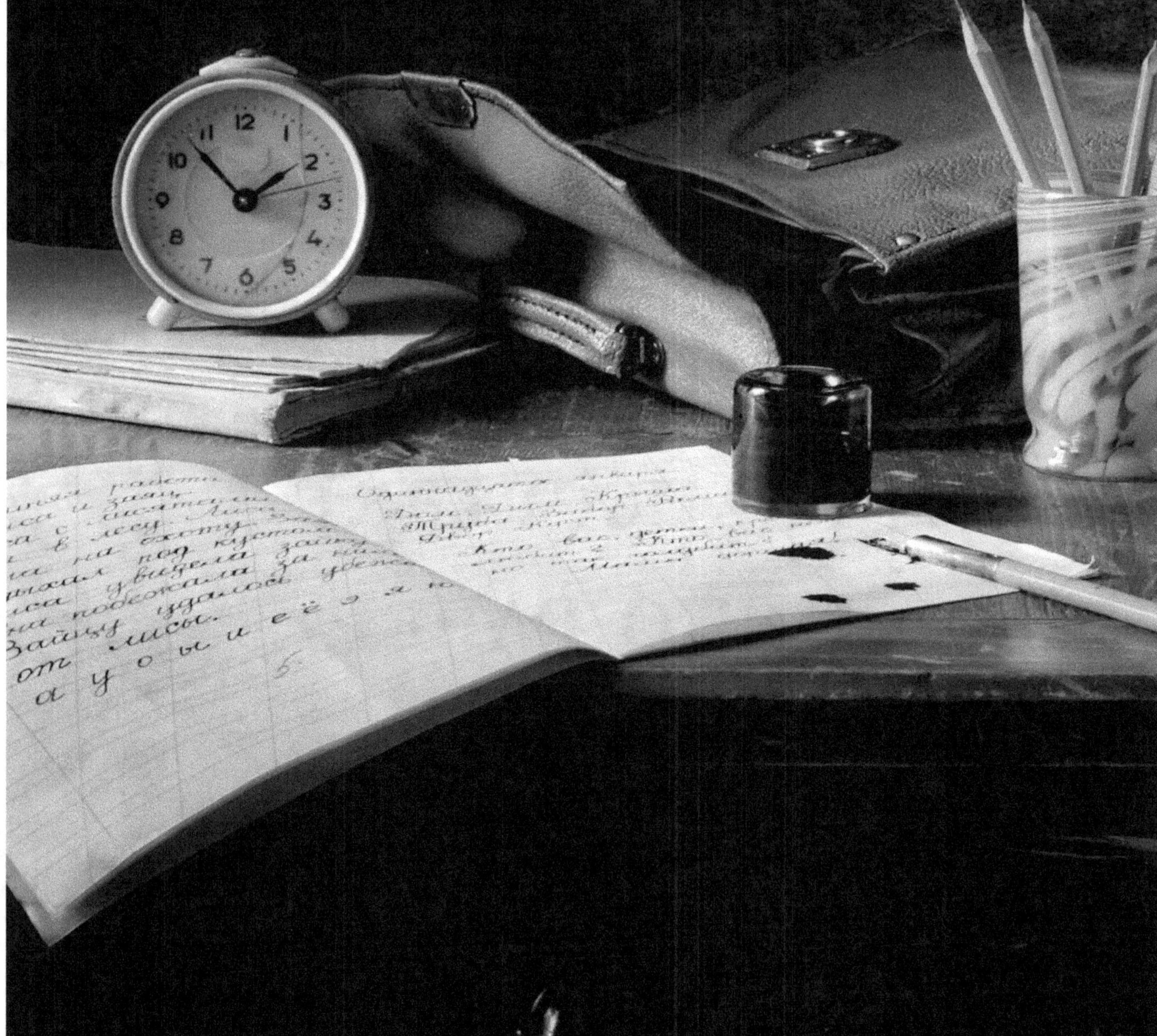

WRITING IS MY CALLING.

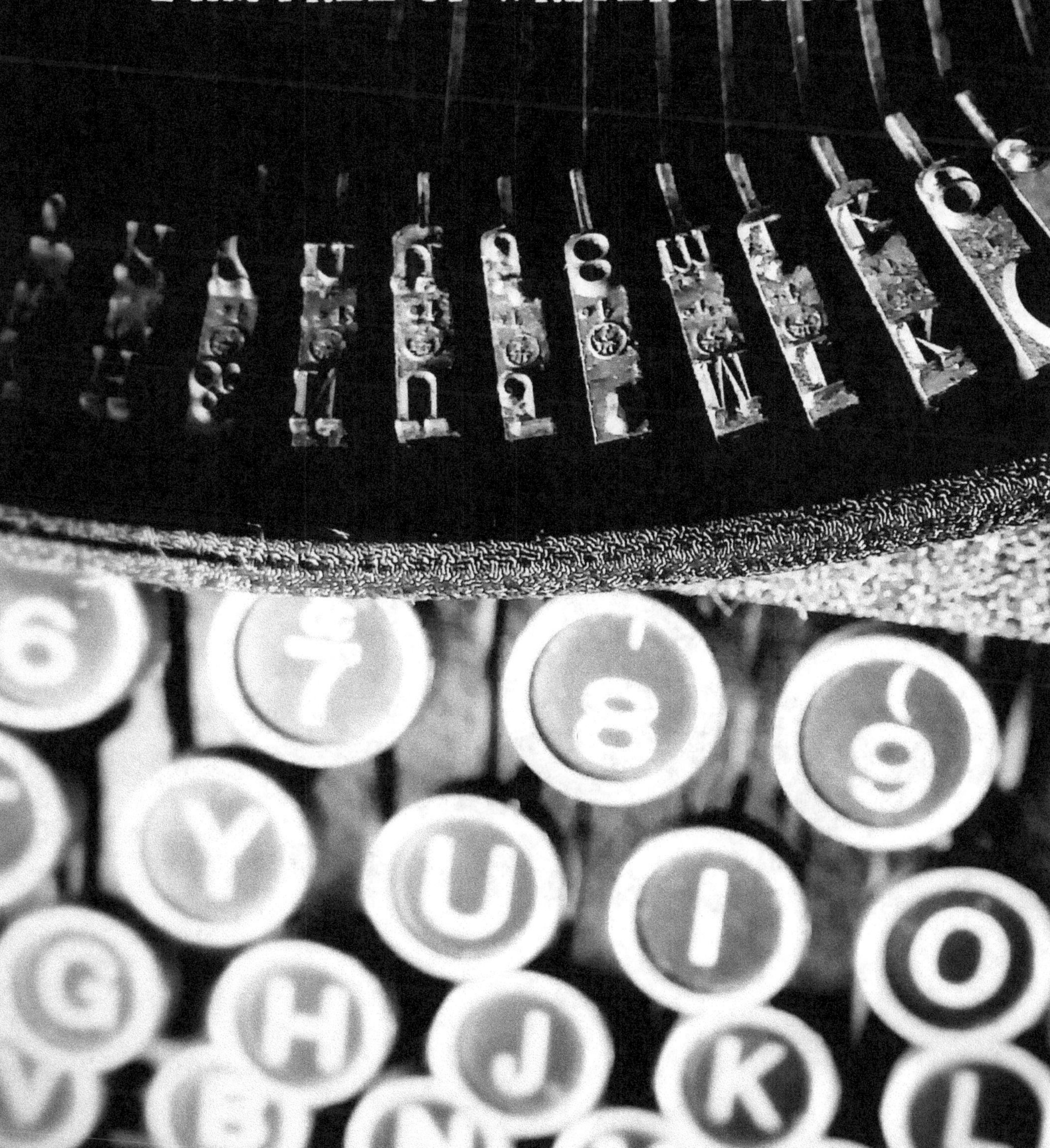

I AM FREE OF WRITER'S BLOCK.

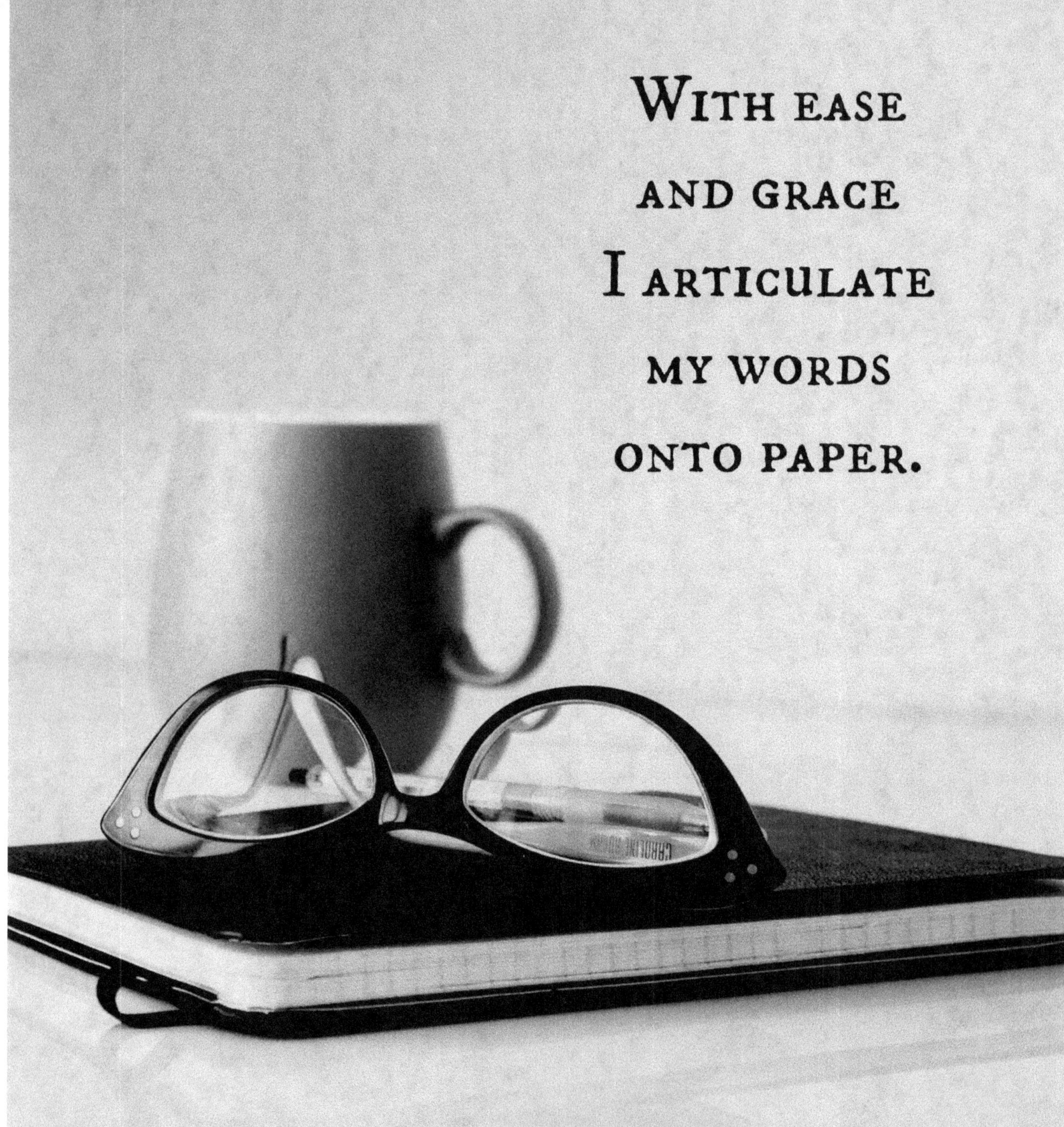
With ease
and grace
I articulate
my words
onto paper.

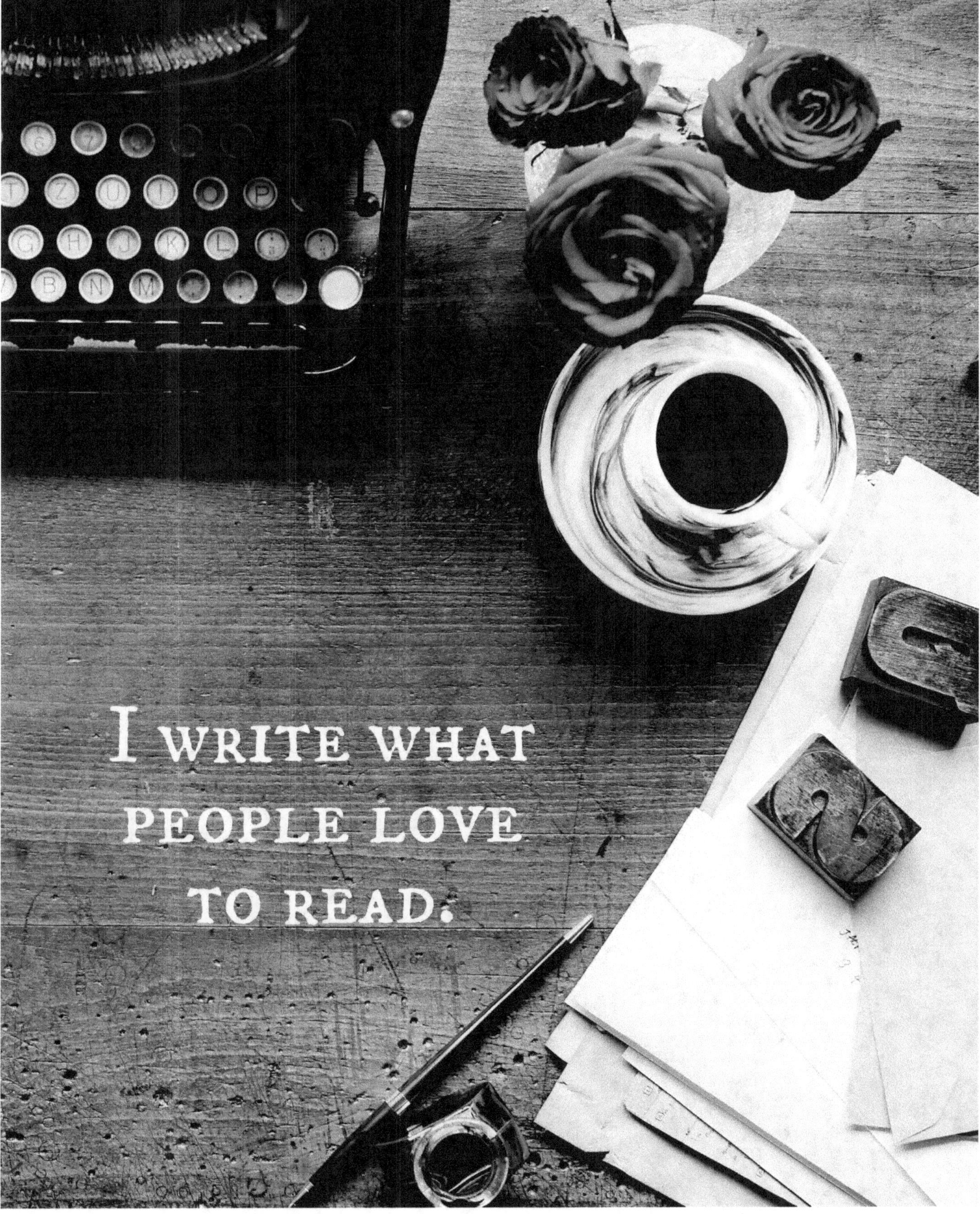

I WRITE WHAT PEOPLE LOVE TO READ.

I FLOW WITH
GENIUS IDEAS
AS I WRITE.

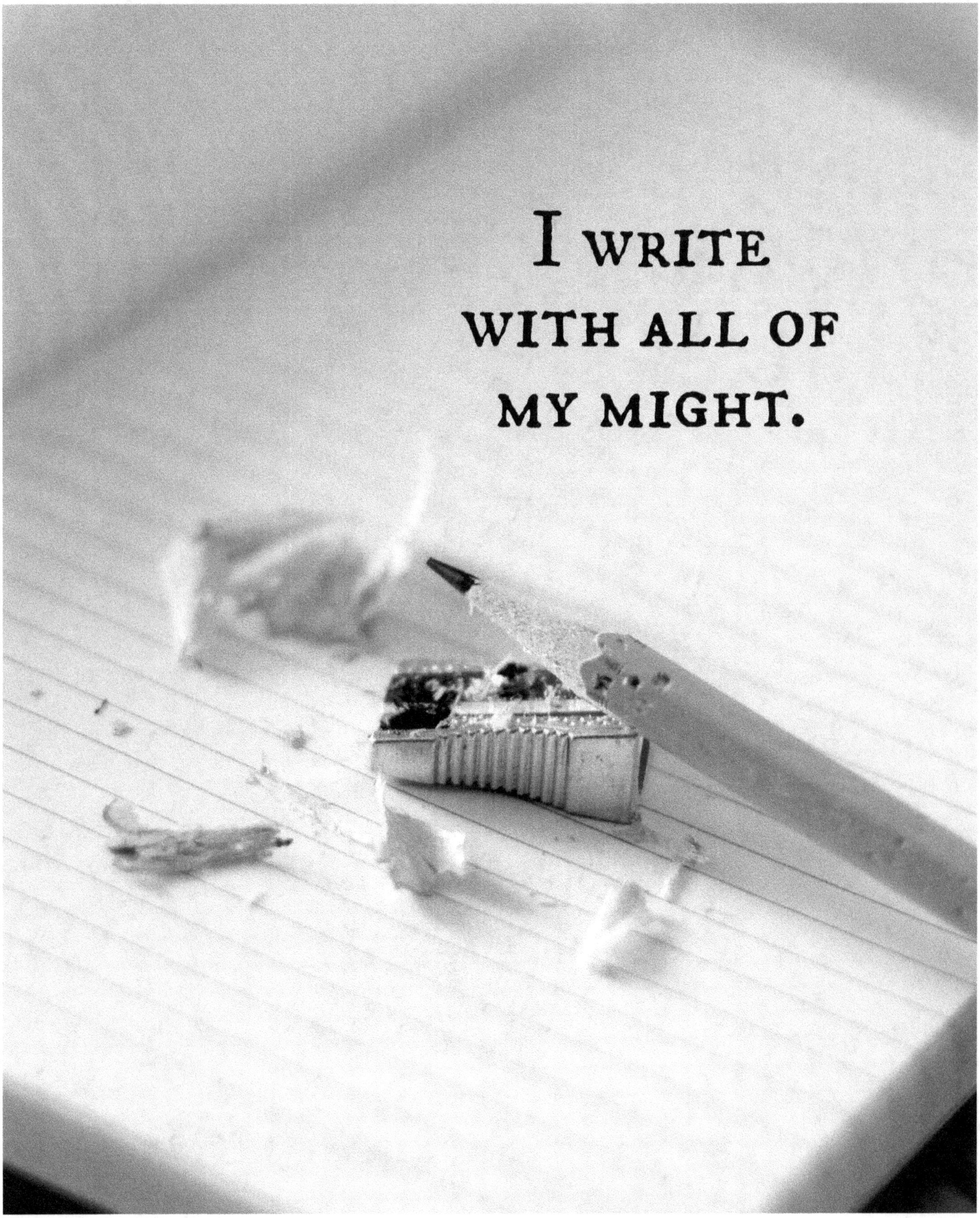

I WRITE
WITH ALL OF
MY MIGHT.

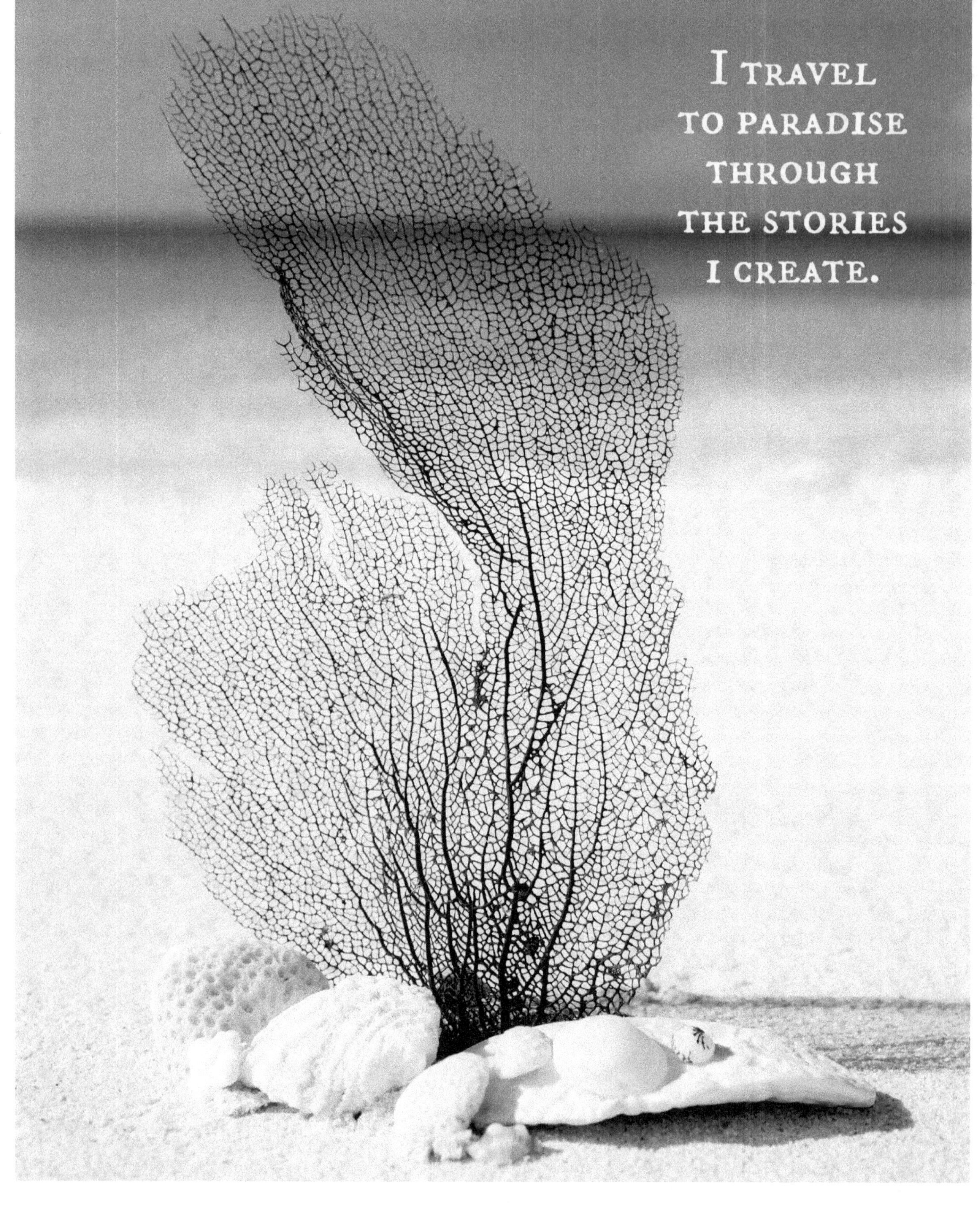
I TRAVEL
TO PARADISE
THROUGH
THE STORIES
I CREATE.

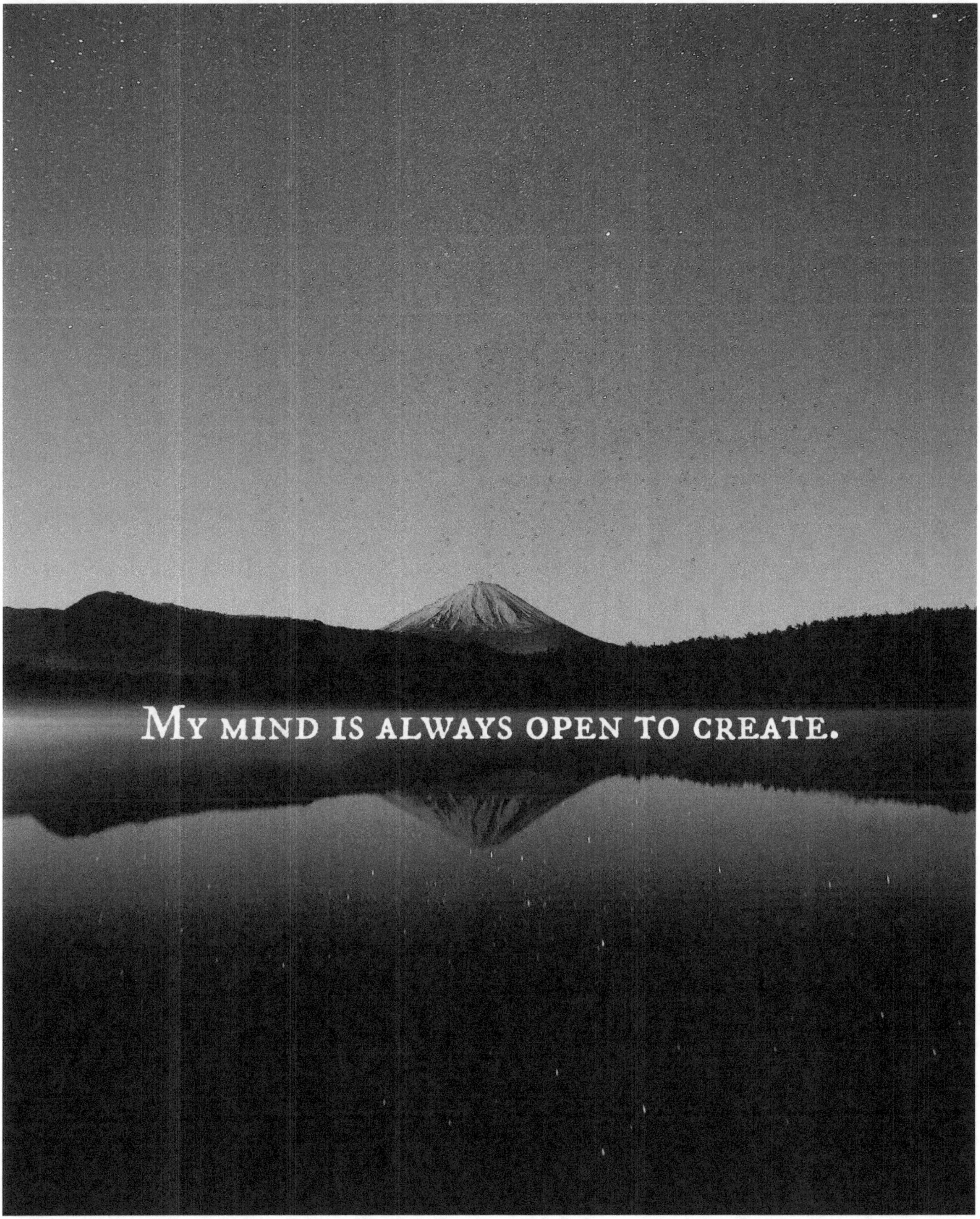

My mind is always open to create.

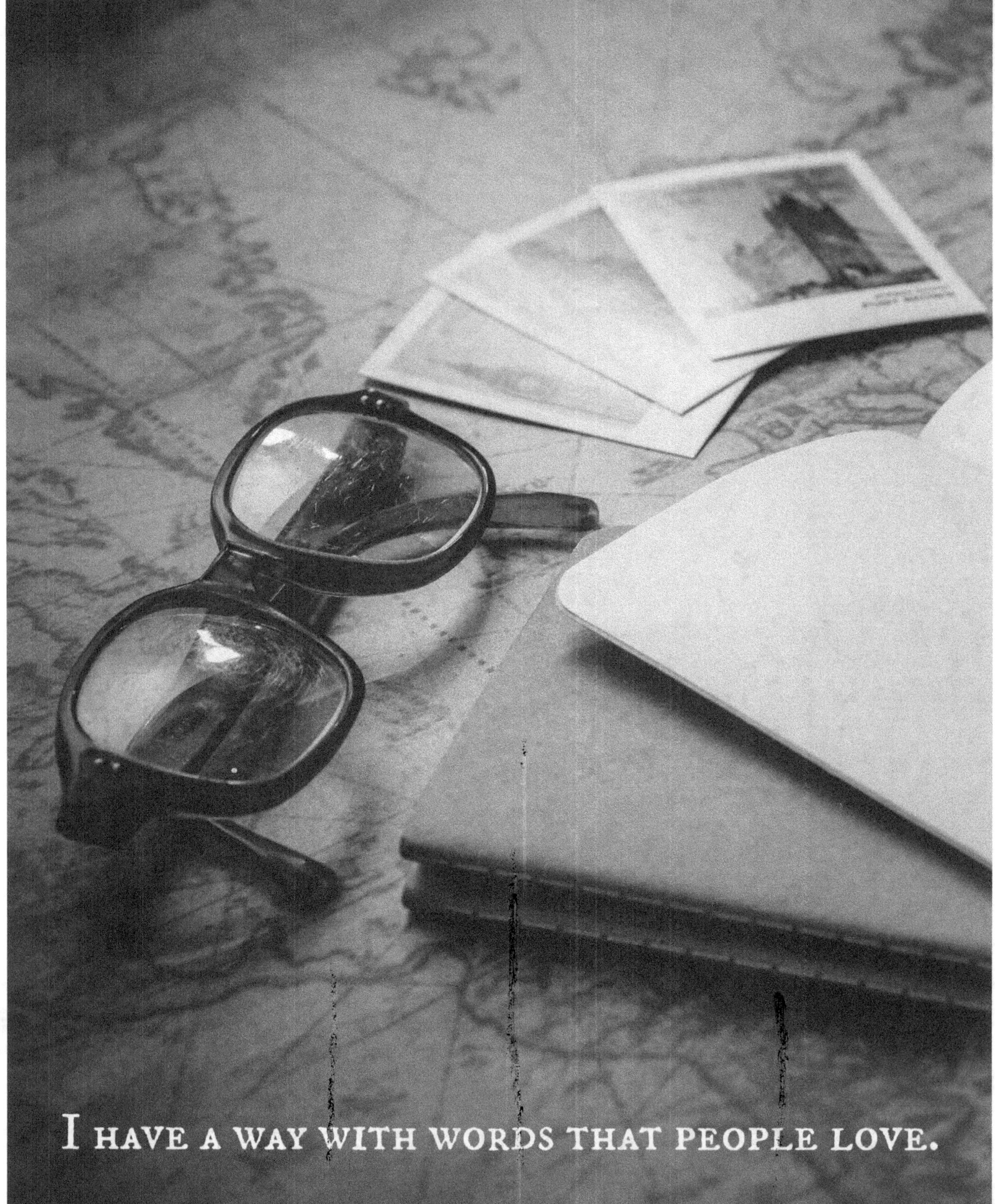
I HAVE A WAY WITH WORDS THAT PEOPLE LOVE.

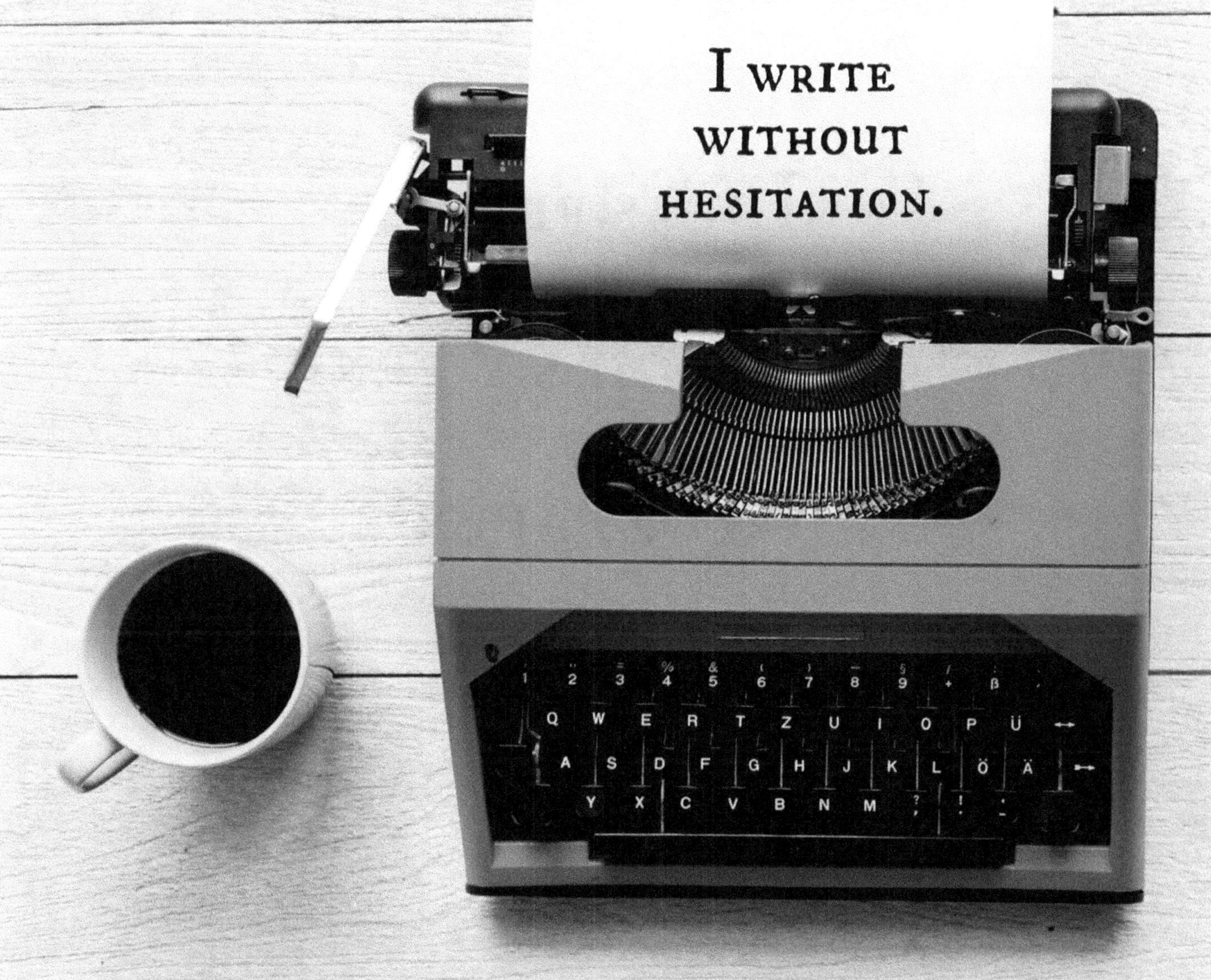

I WRITE
WITHOUT
HESITATION.

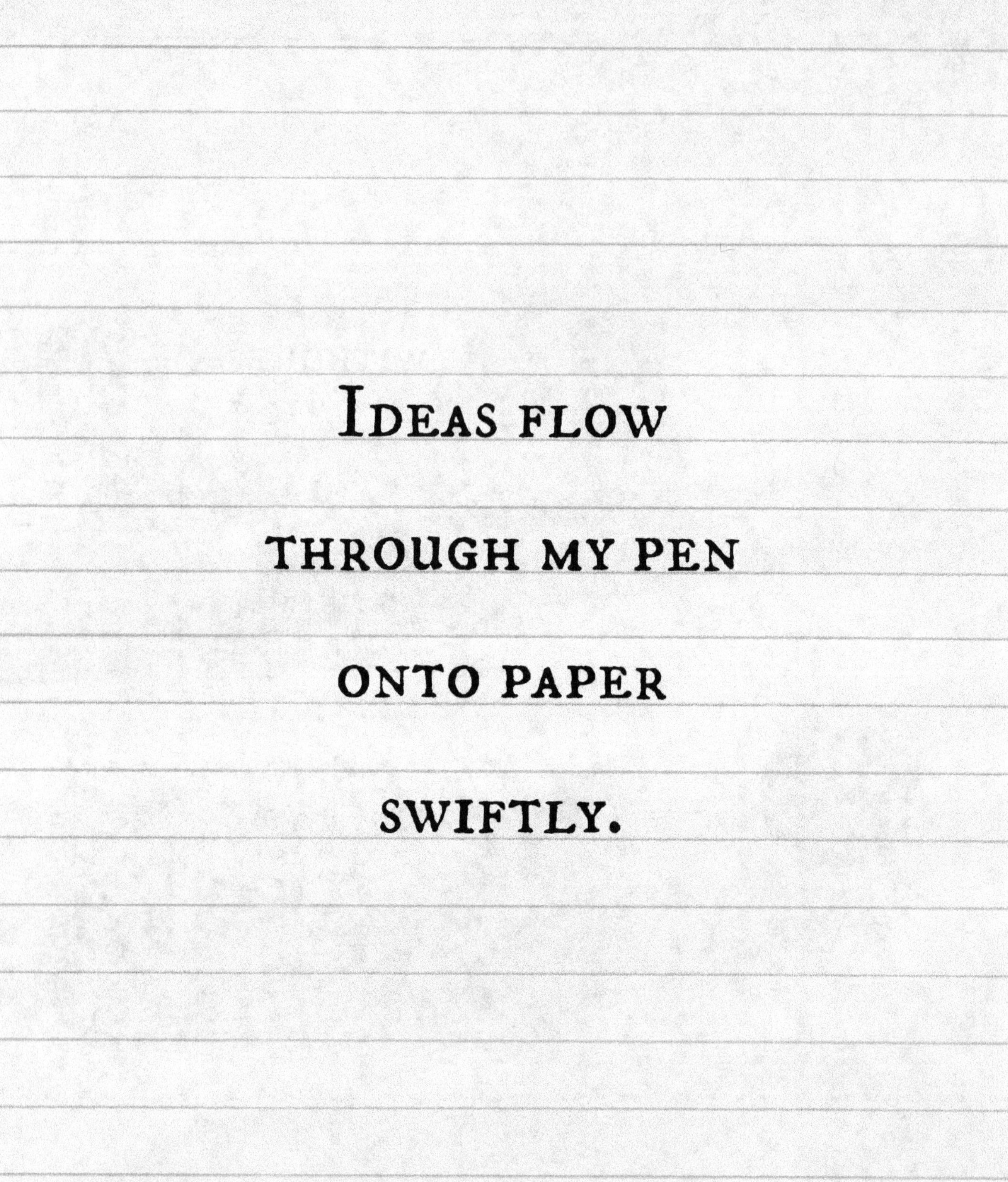

IDEAS FLOW
THROUGH MY PEN
ONTO PAPER
SWIFTLY.

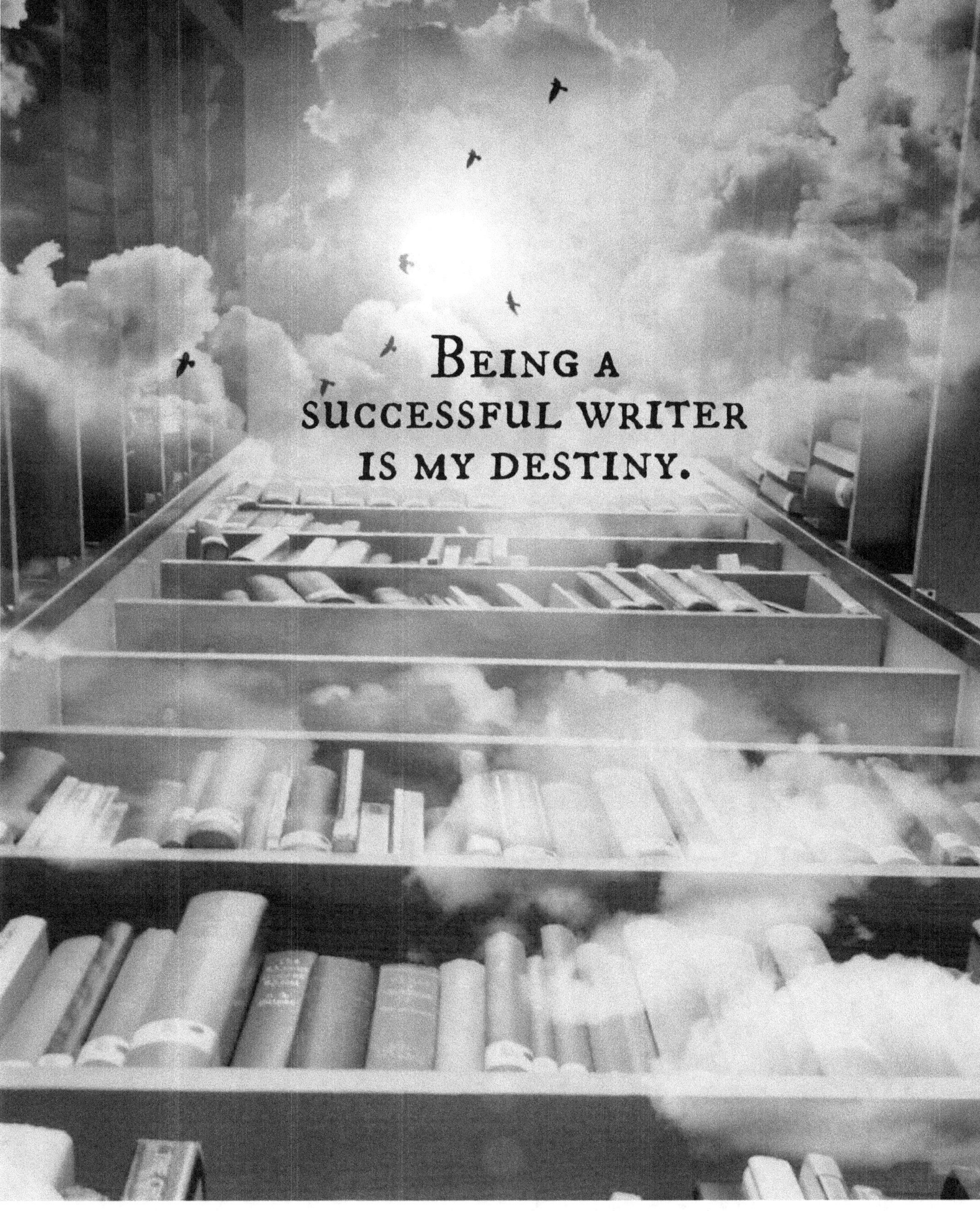

BEING A
SUCCESSFUL WRITER
IS MY DESTINY.

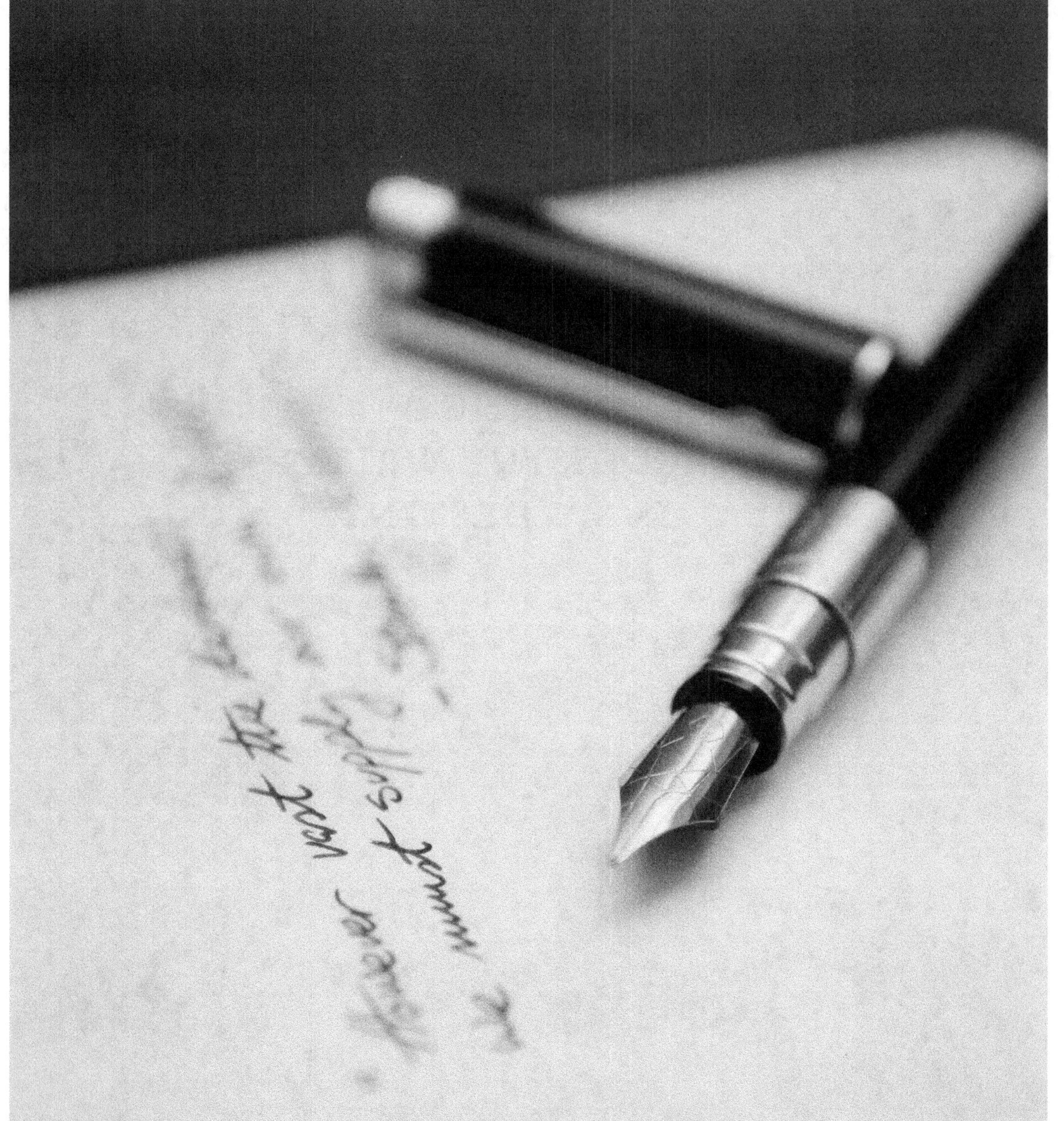

WRITING IS WHAT I AM MEANT TO DO.

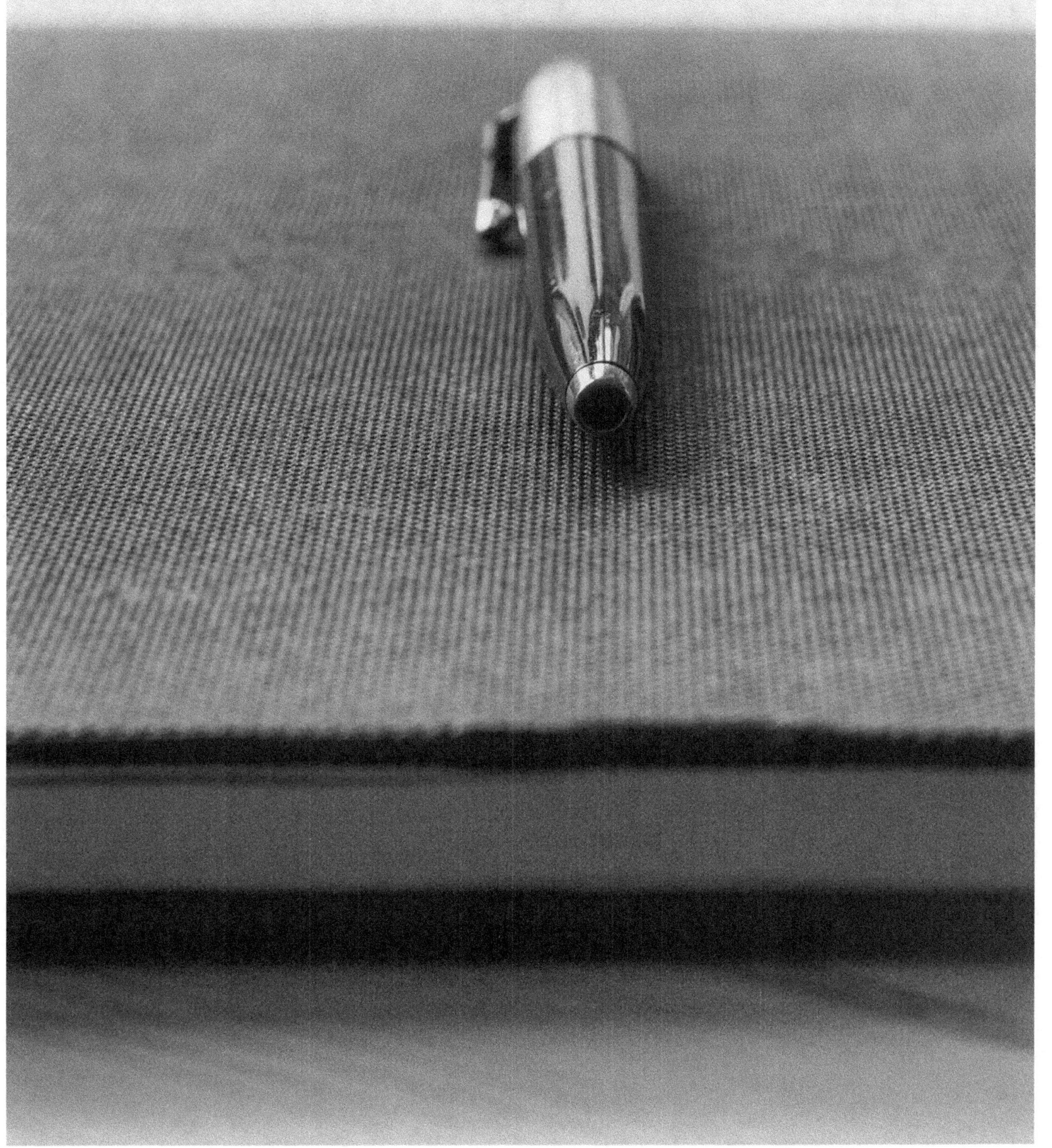

I WRITE EVERYDAY.

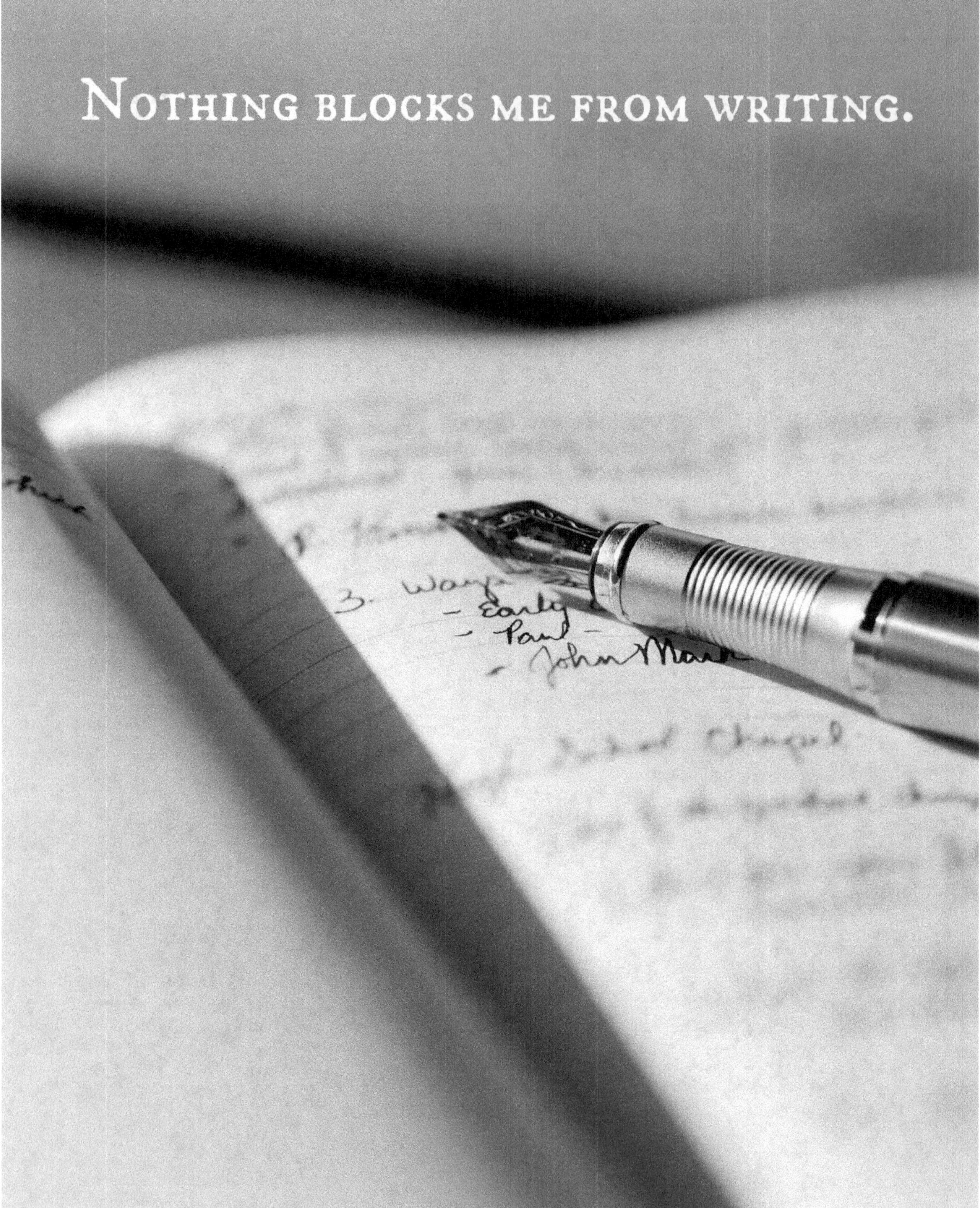
NOTHING BLOCKS ME FROM WRITING.

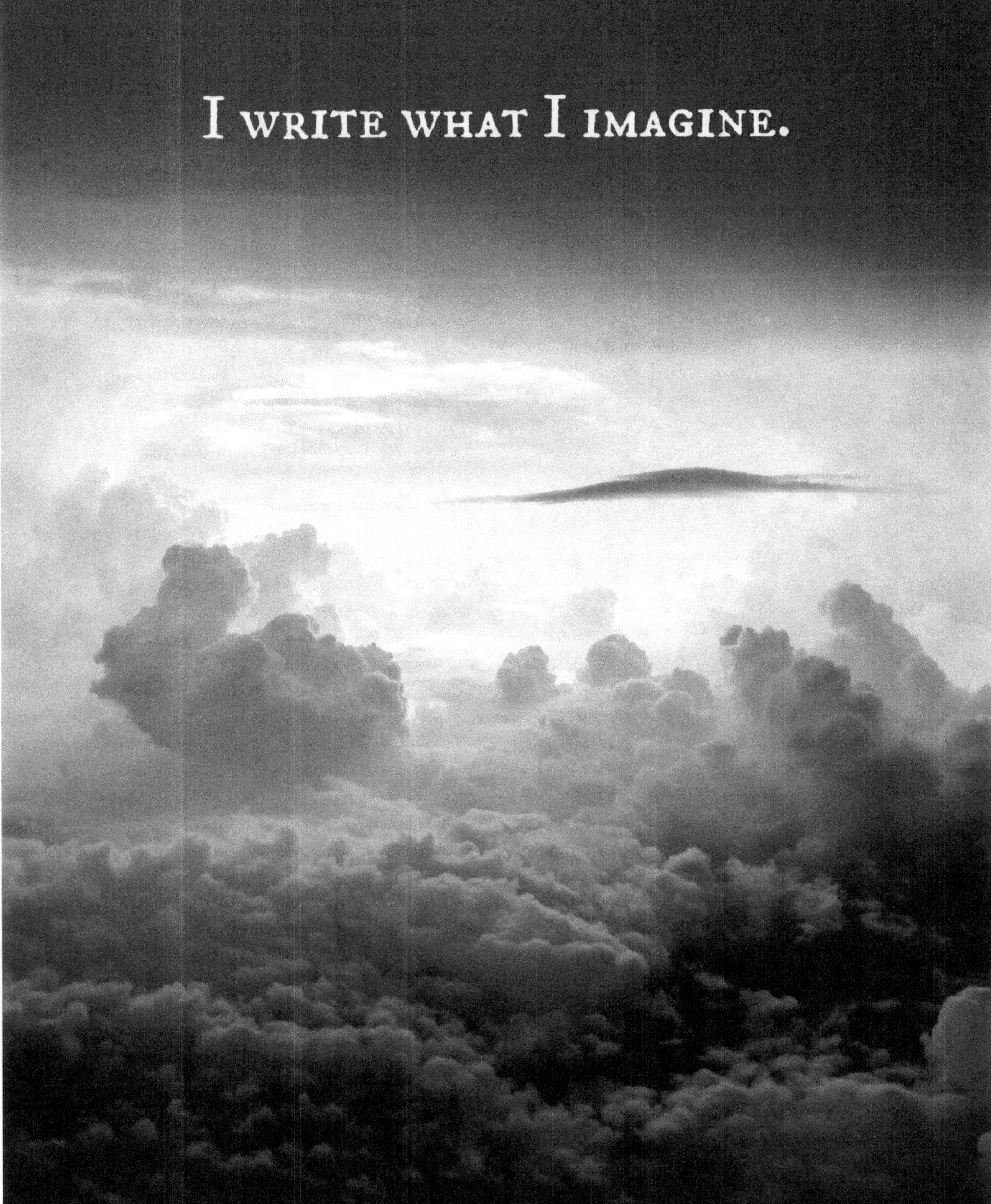
I WRITE WHAT I IMAGINE.

I AM ABUNDANT IN IDEAS.

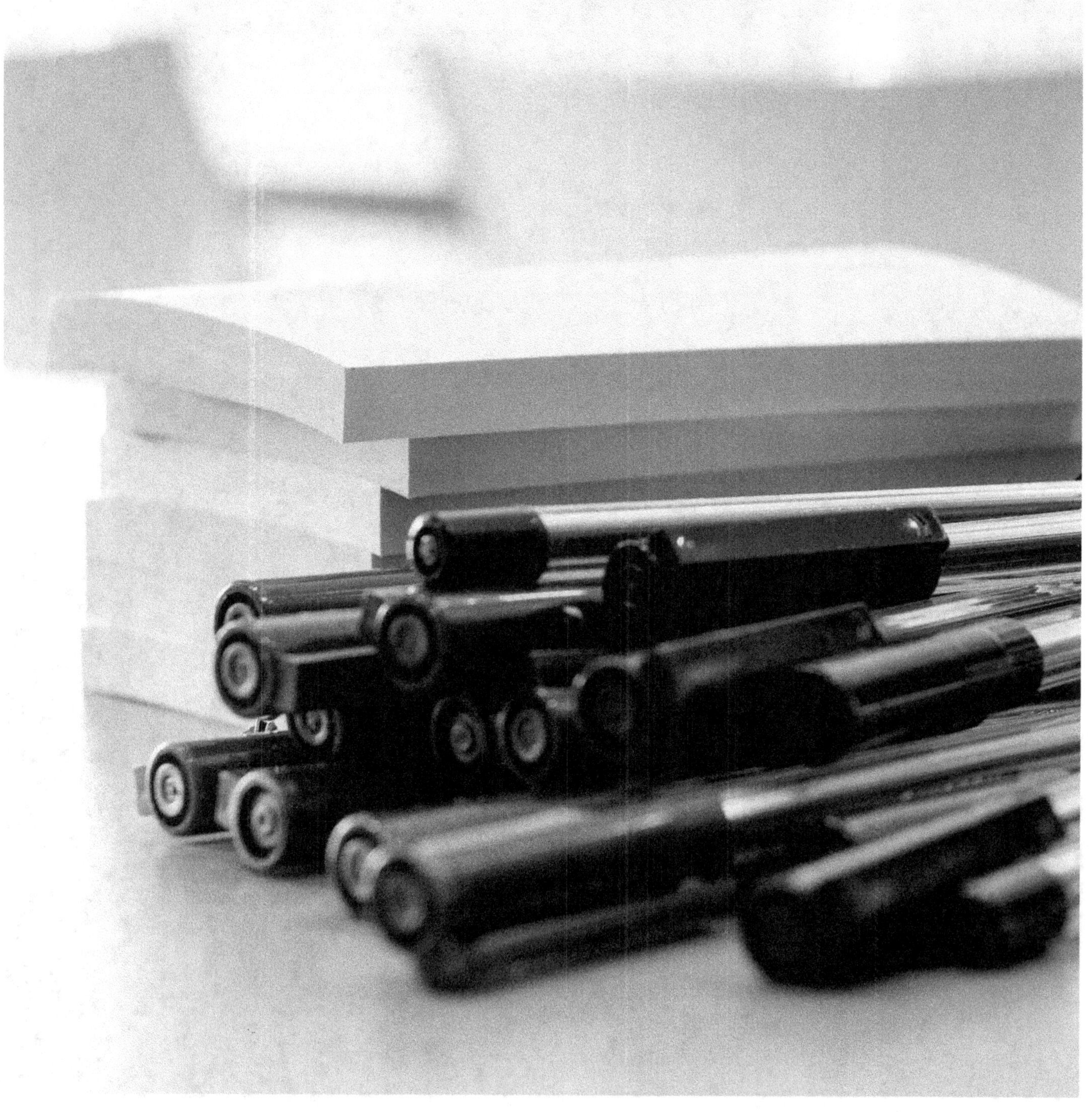

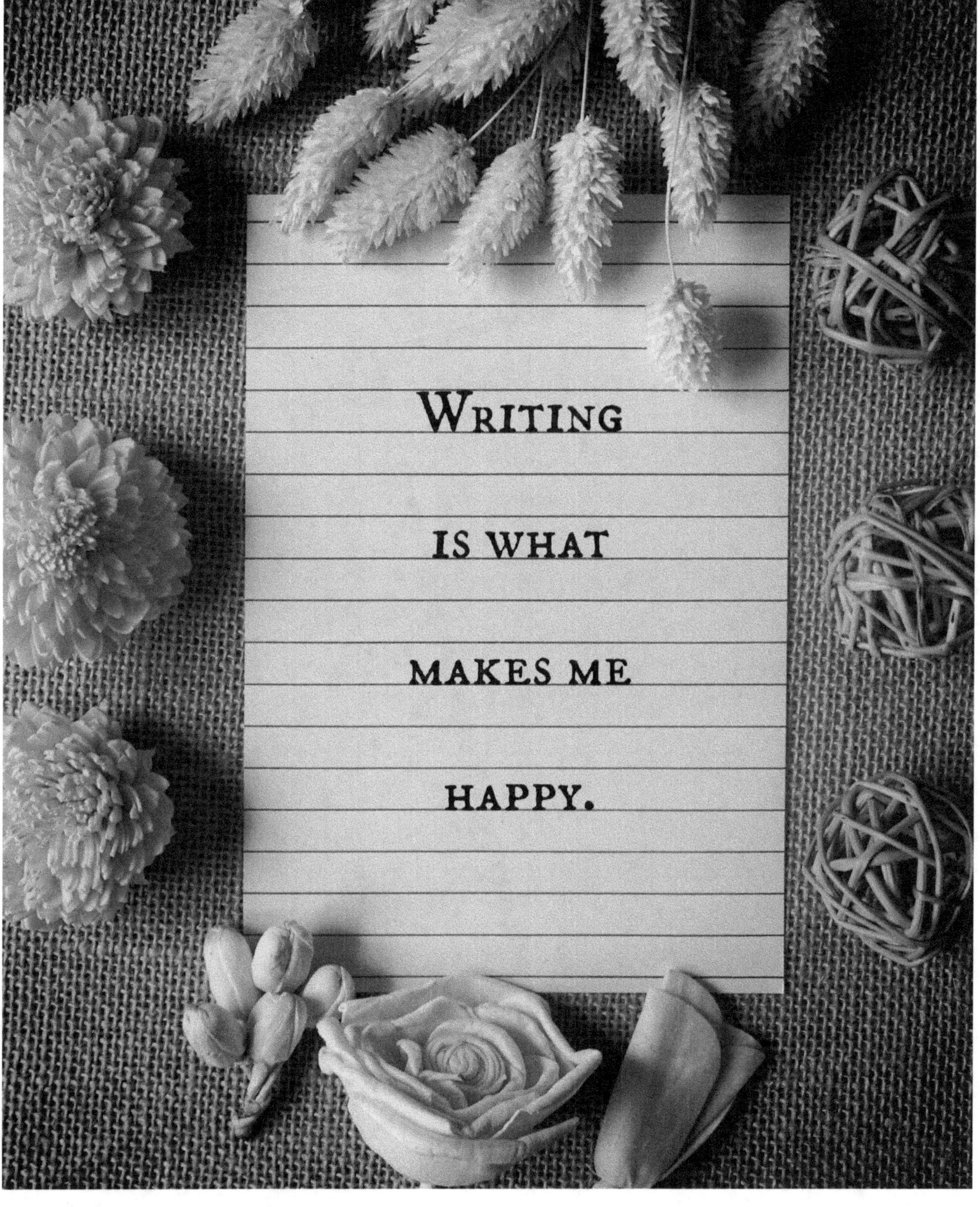

WRITING
IS WHAT
MAKES ME
HAPPY.

I LIVE TO WRITE.

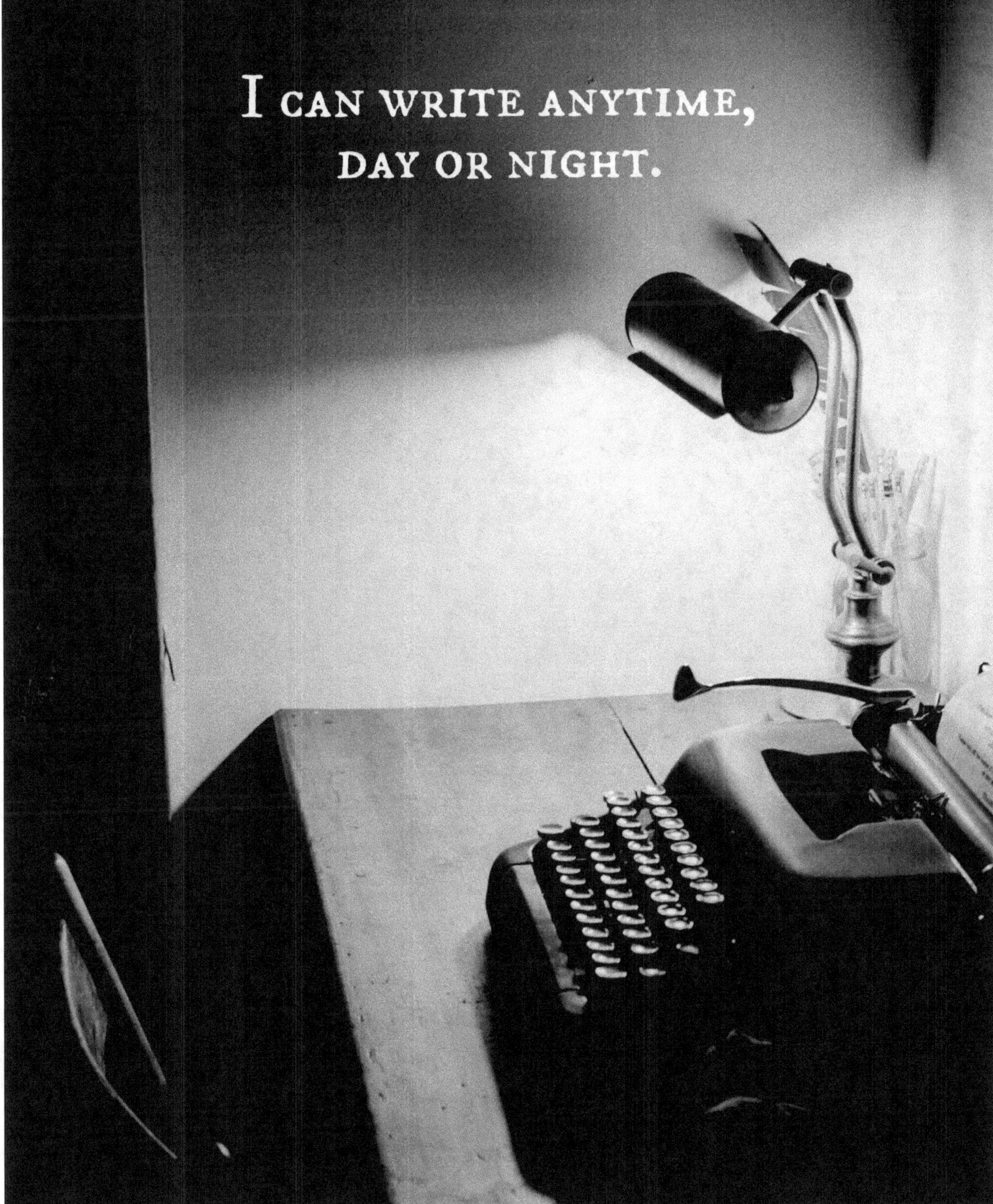
I CAN WRITE ANYTIME, DAY OR NIGHT.

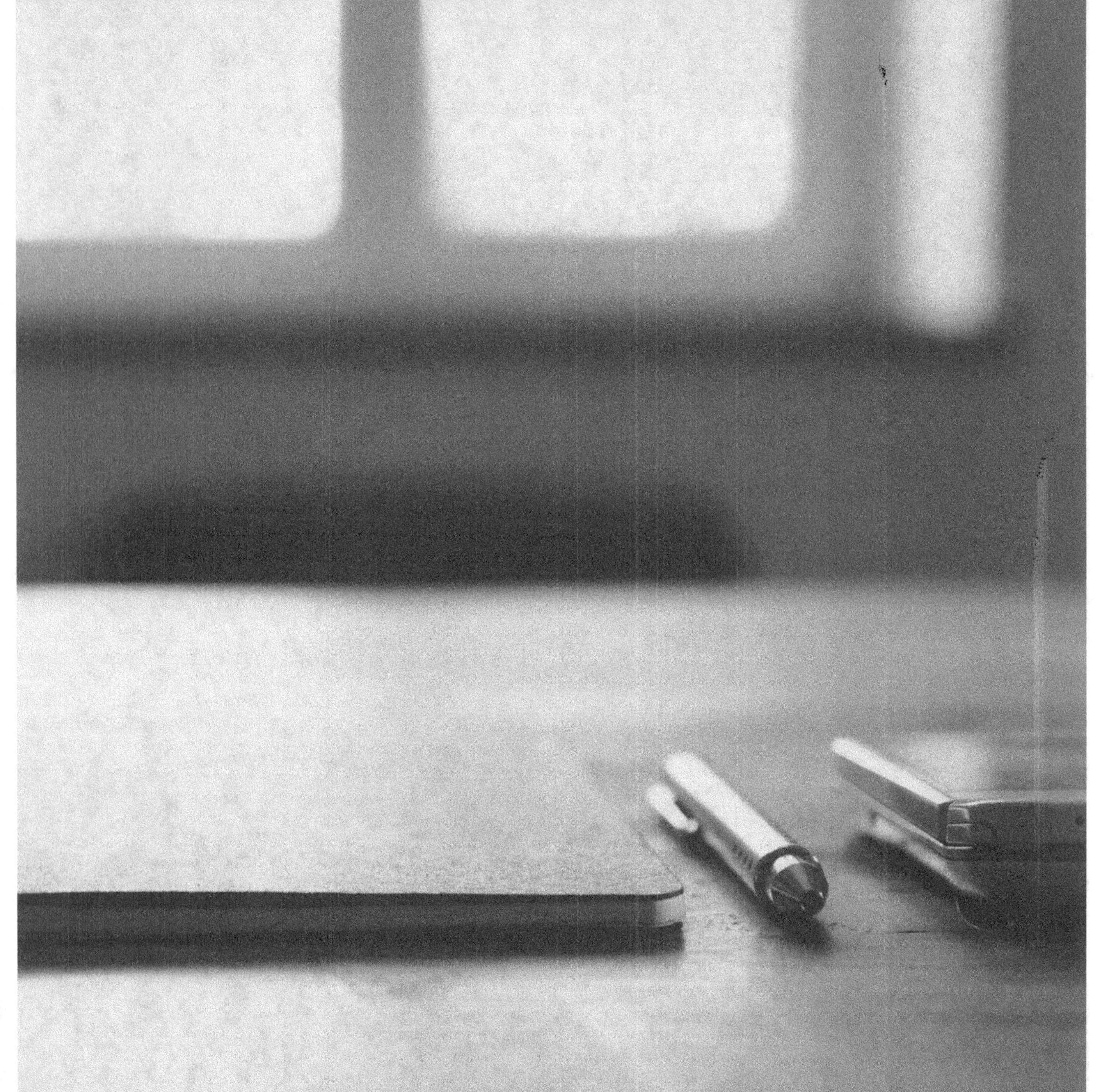

WRITER'S BLOCK DOESN'T AFFECT ME.

I WRITE
WHAT I
OBSERVE.

I write to thrive.

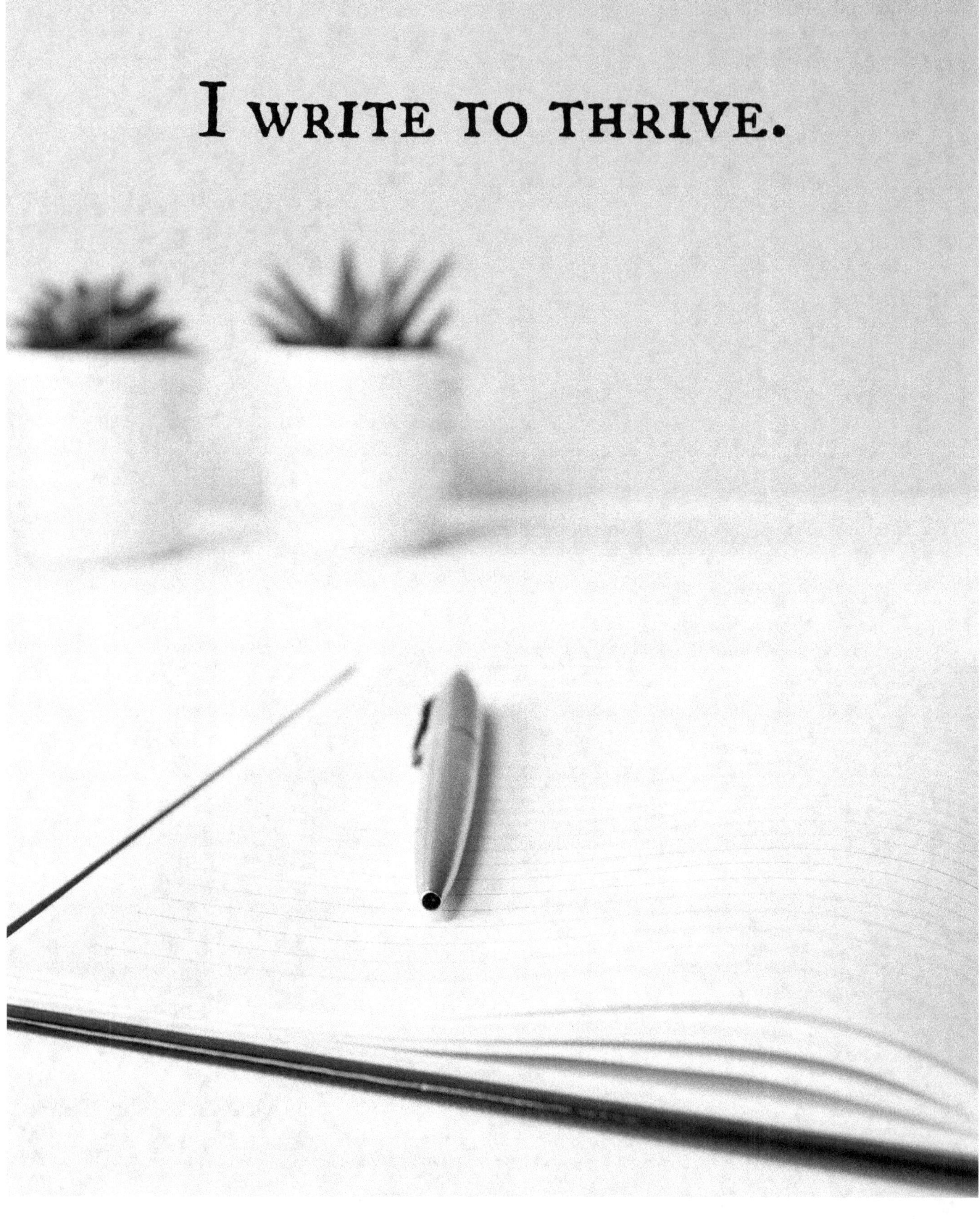

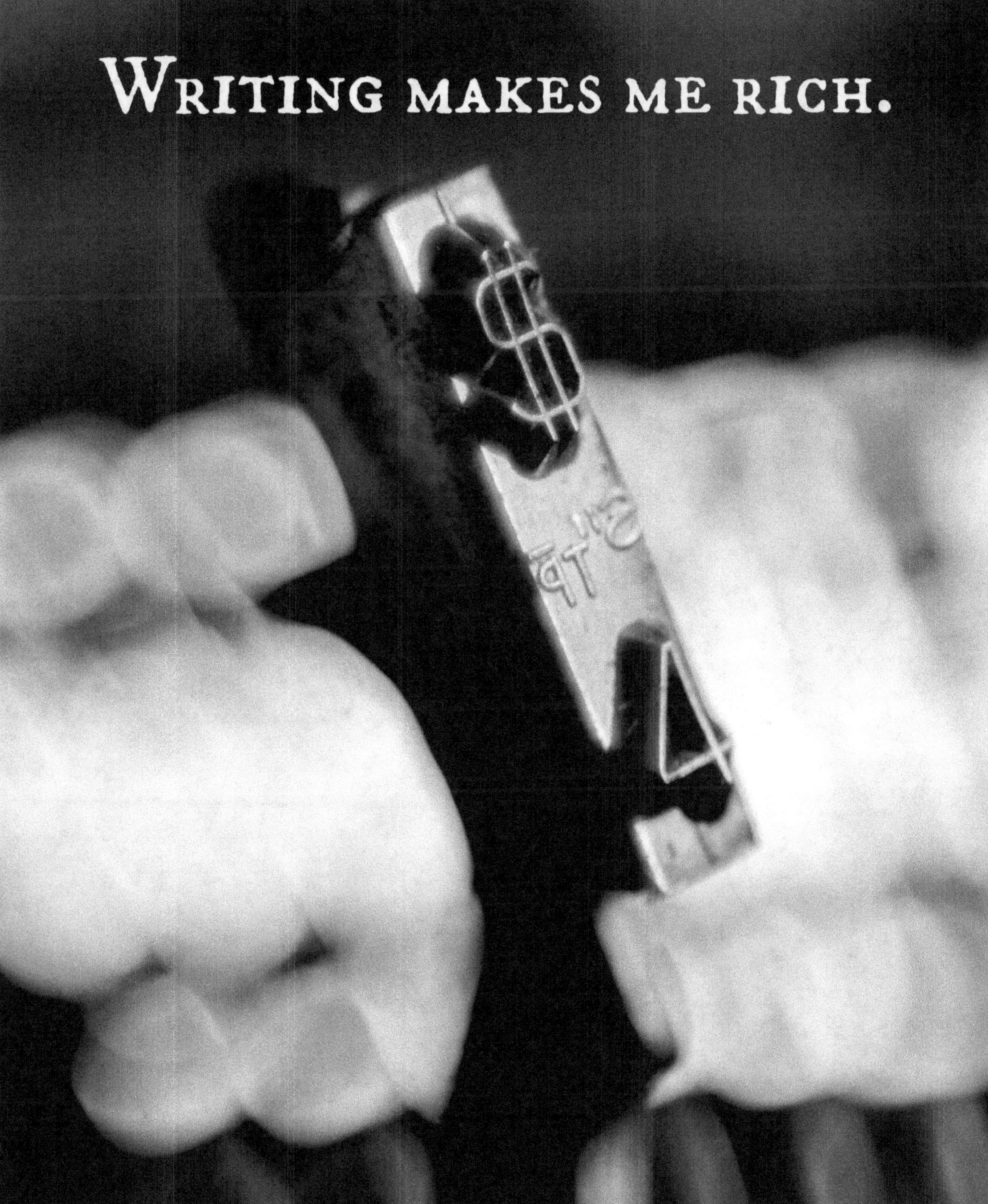# Writing makes me rich.

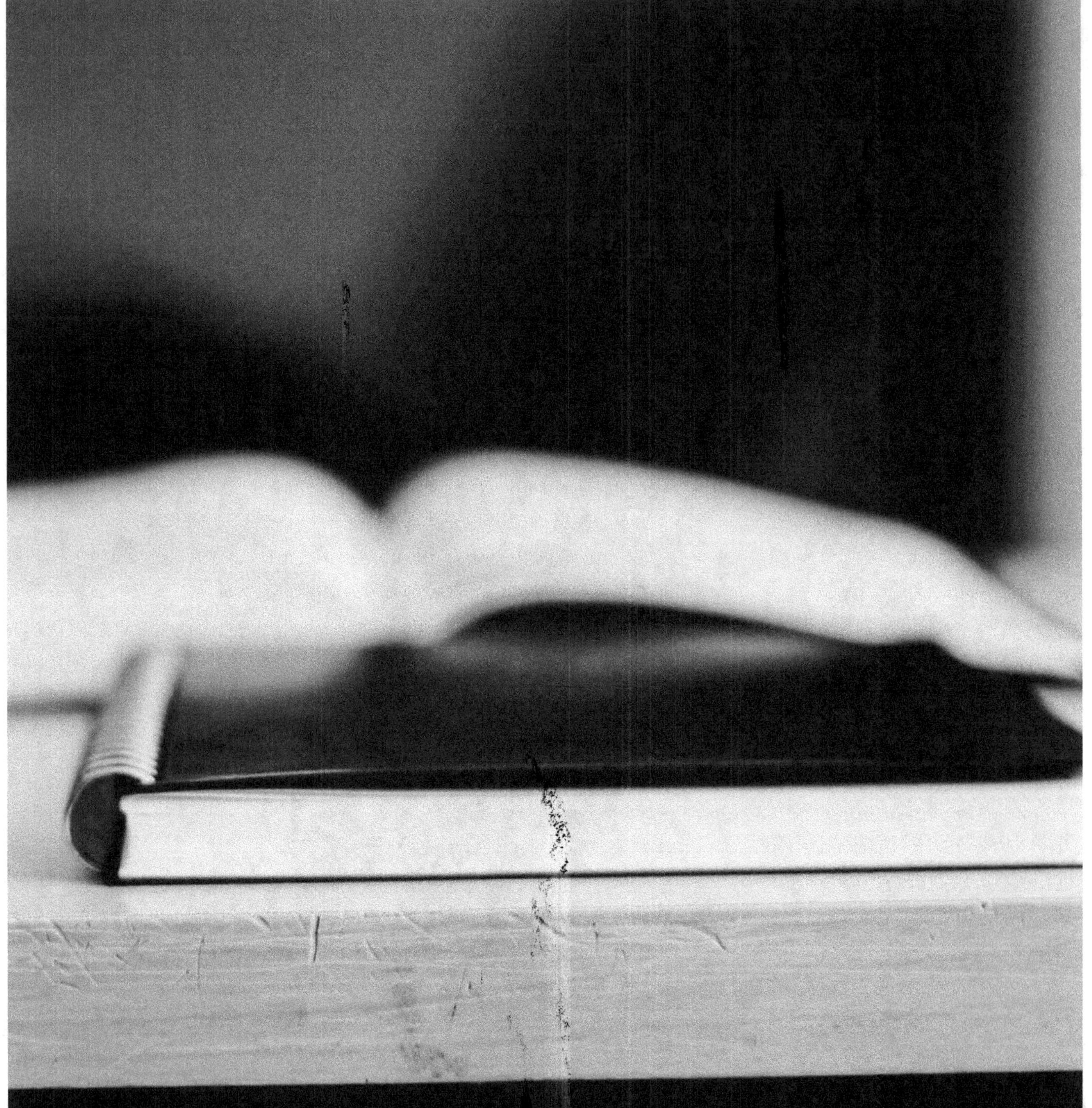
I WRITE WHAT I LEARN.

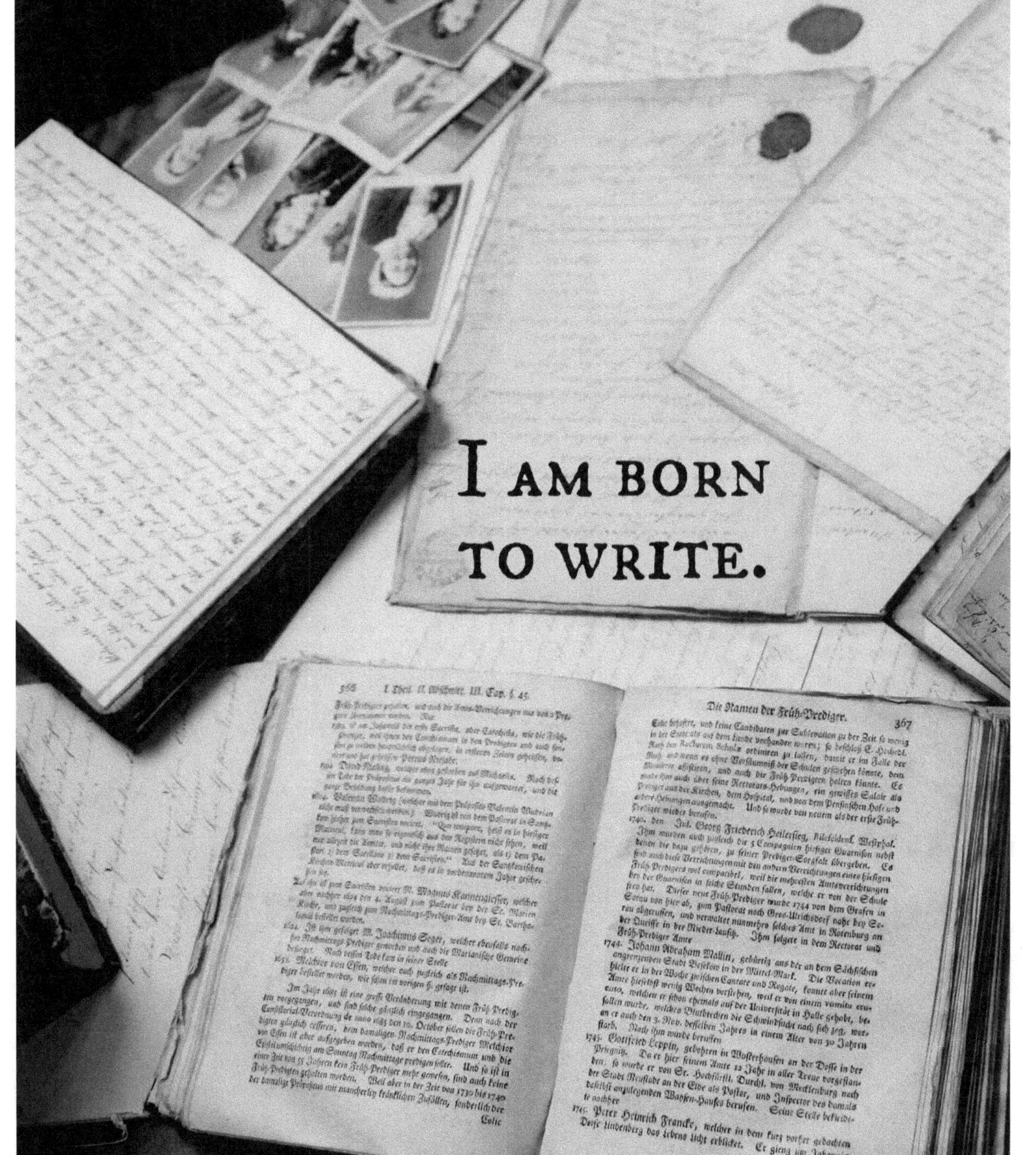
I AM BORN TO WRITE.

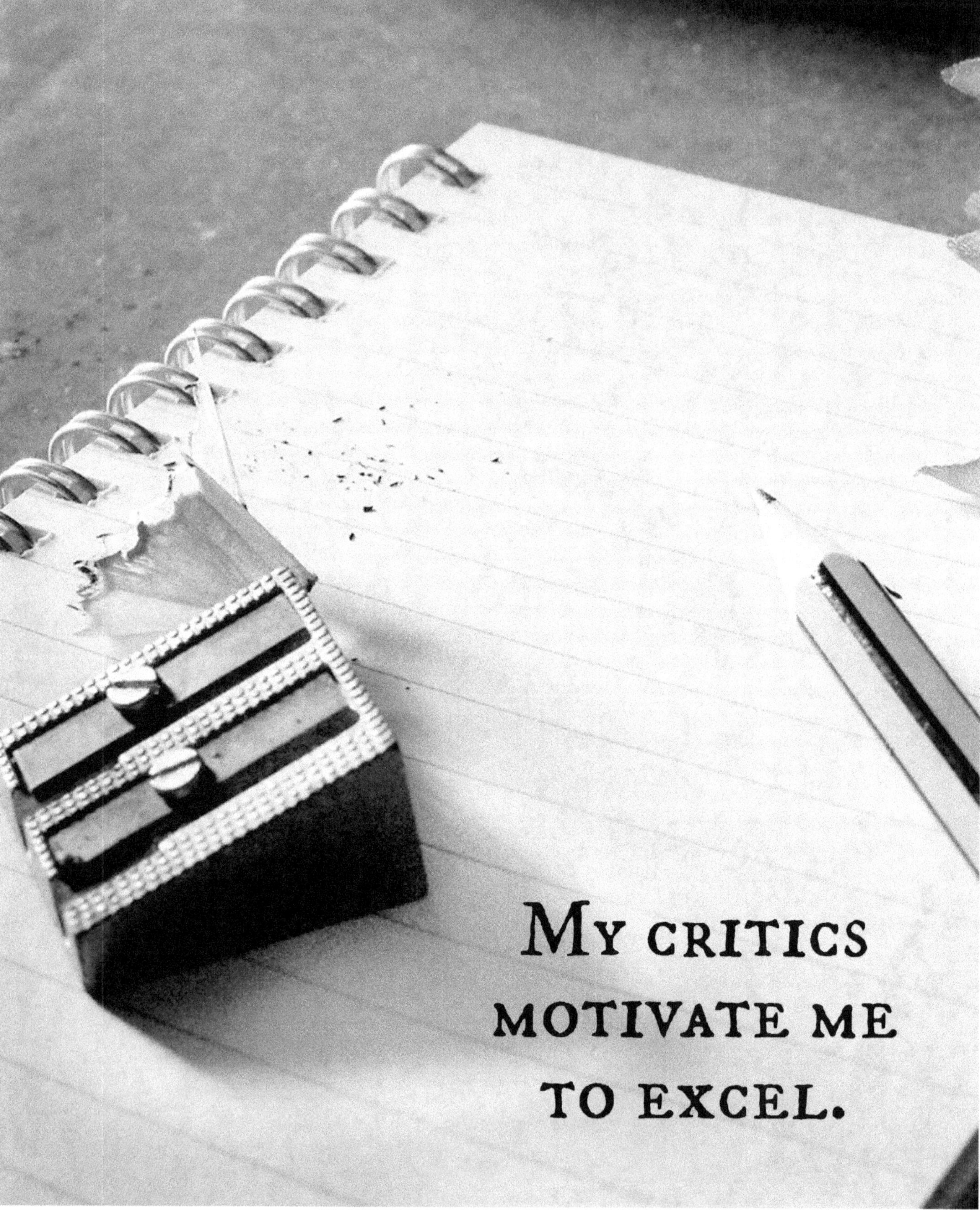
MY CRITICS
MOTIVATE ME
TO EXCEL.

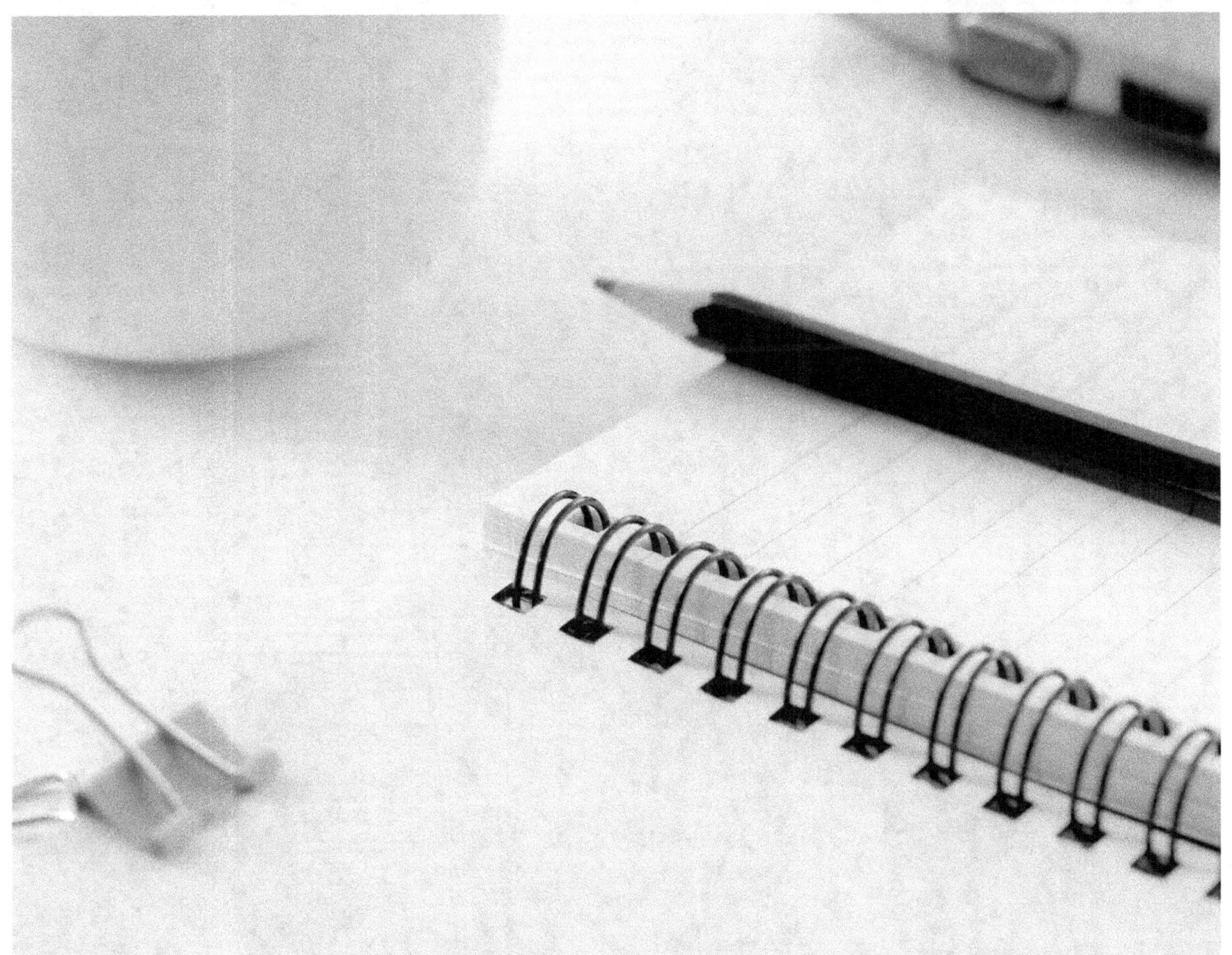

I AM COMMITTED
TO WRITE EVERY DAY.

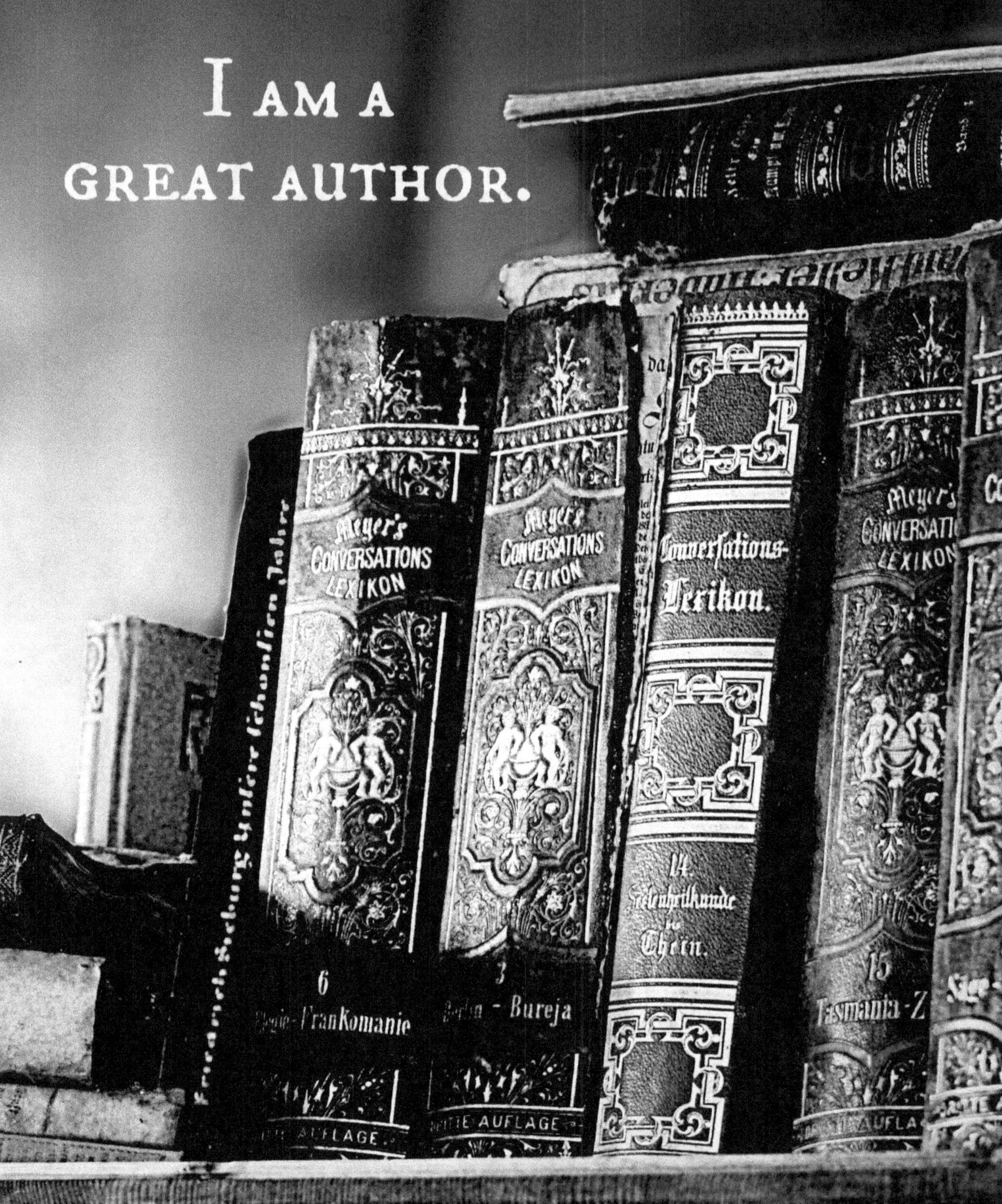

I AM A GREAT AUTHOR.

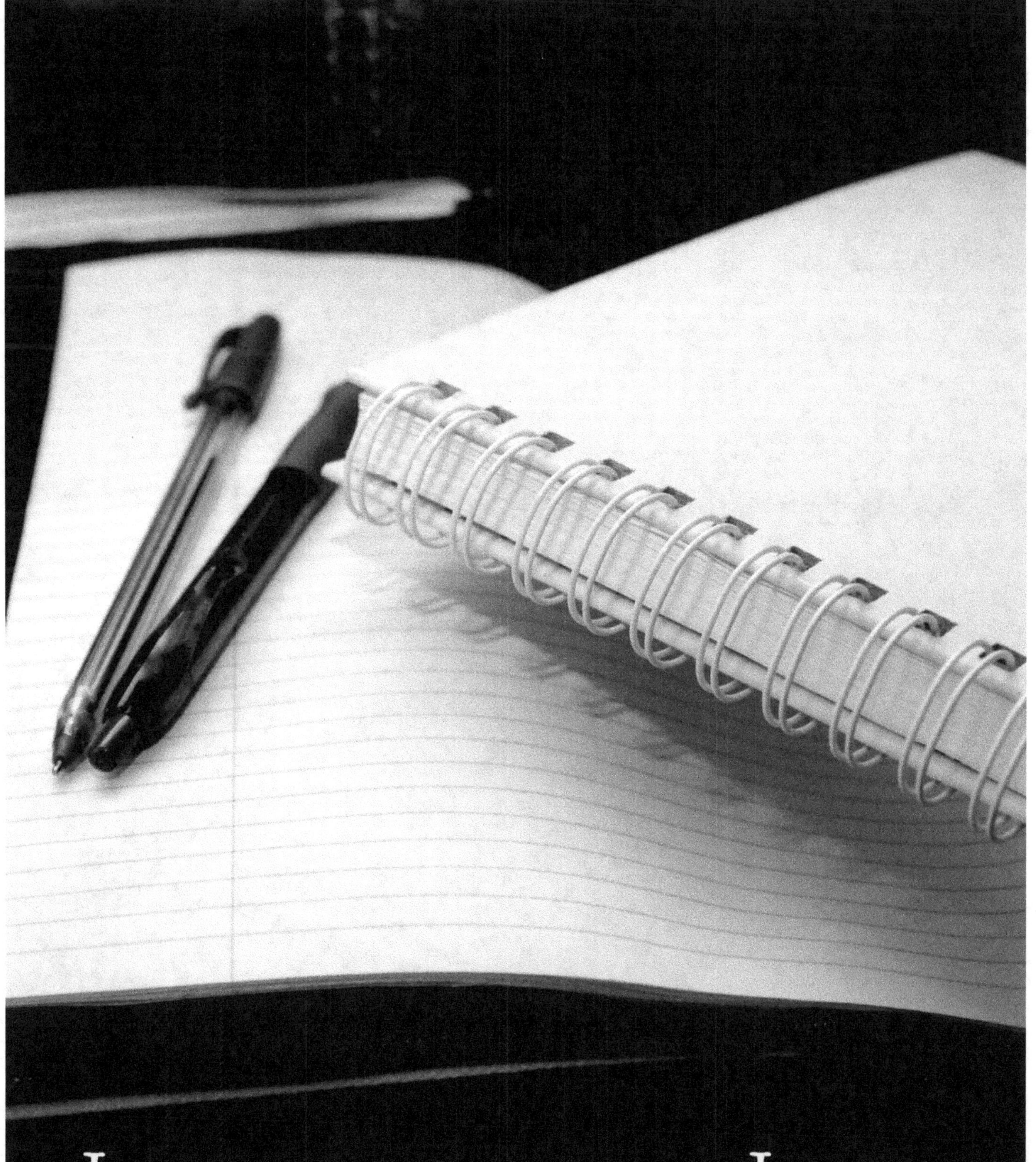

I AM NEVER BORED BECAUSE I WRITE.

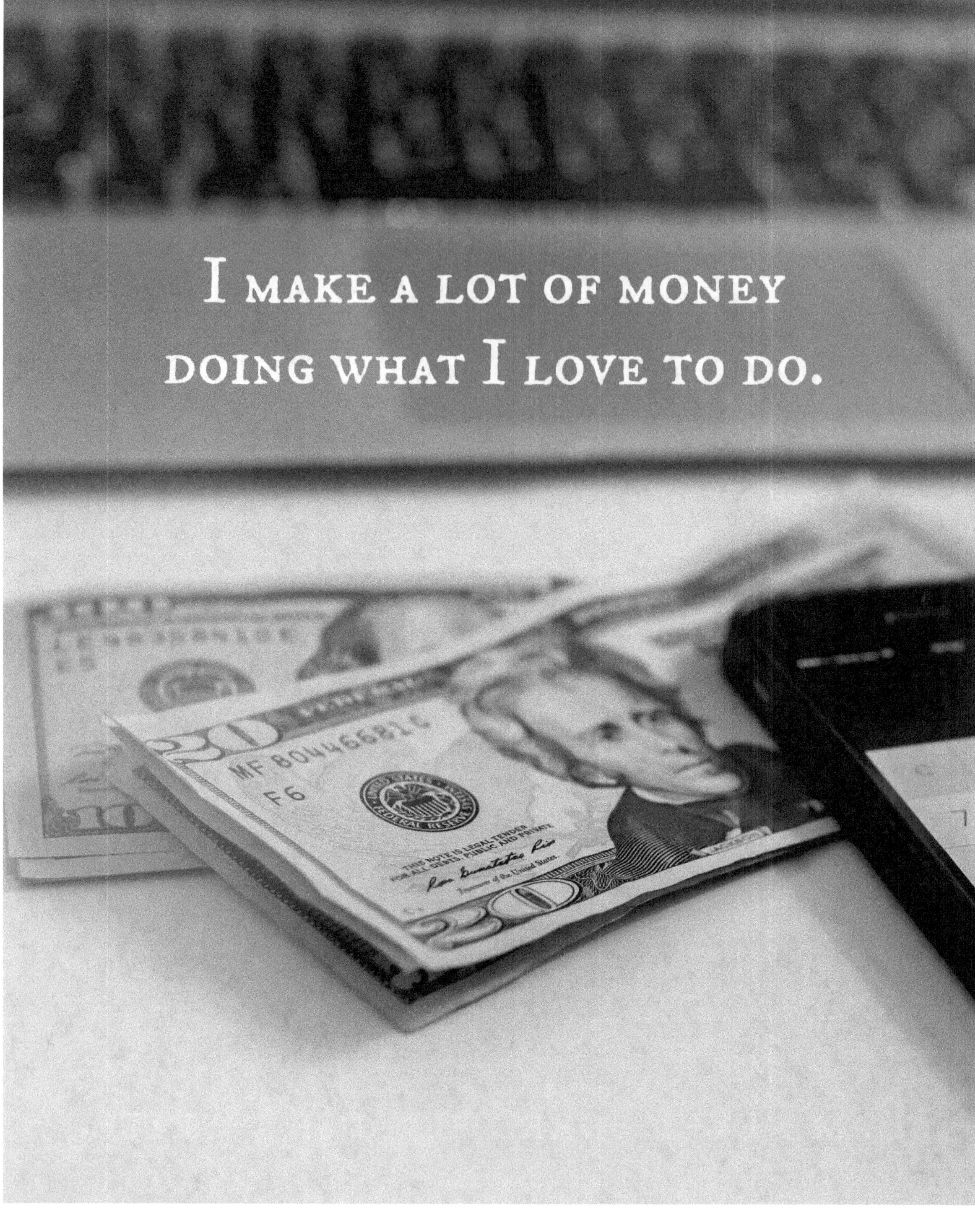

I make a lot of money doing what I love to do.

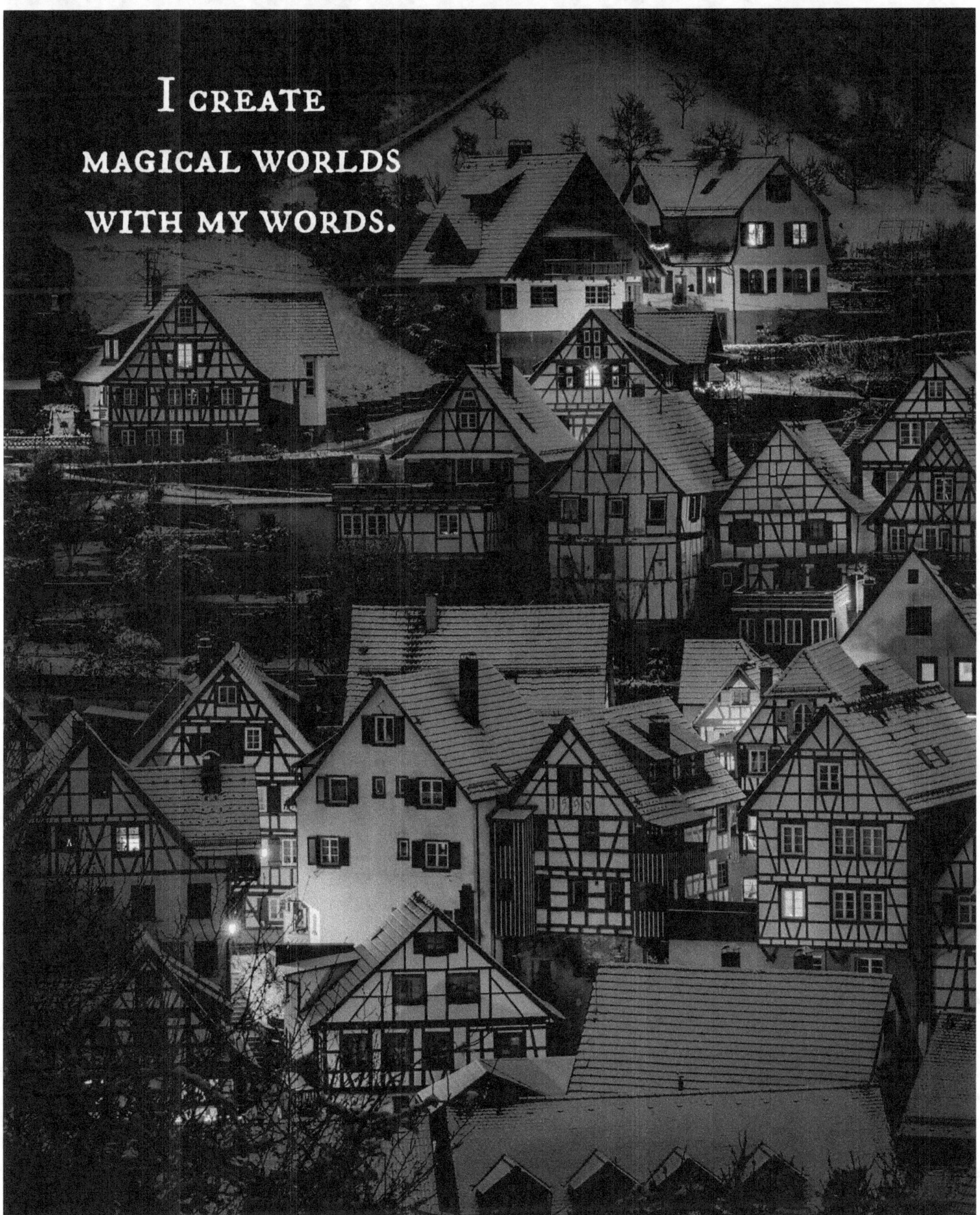
I CREATE
MAGICAL WORLDS
WITH MY WORDS.

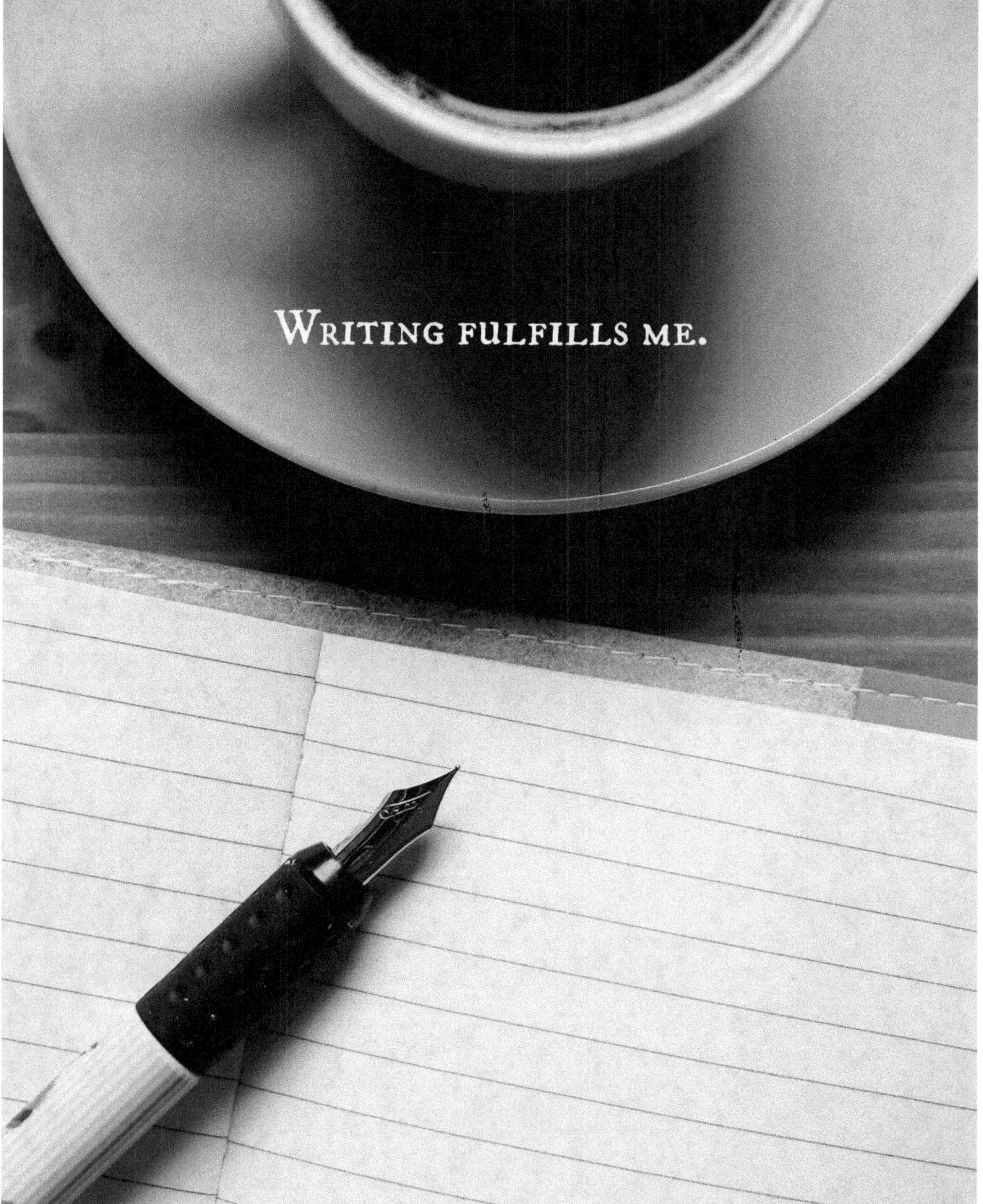
WRITING FULFILLS ME.

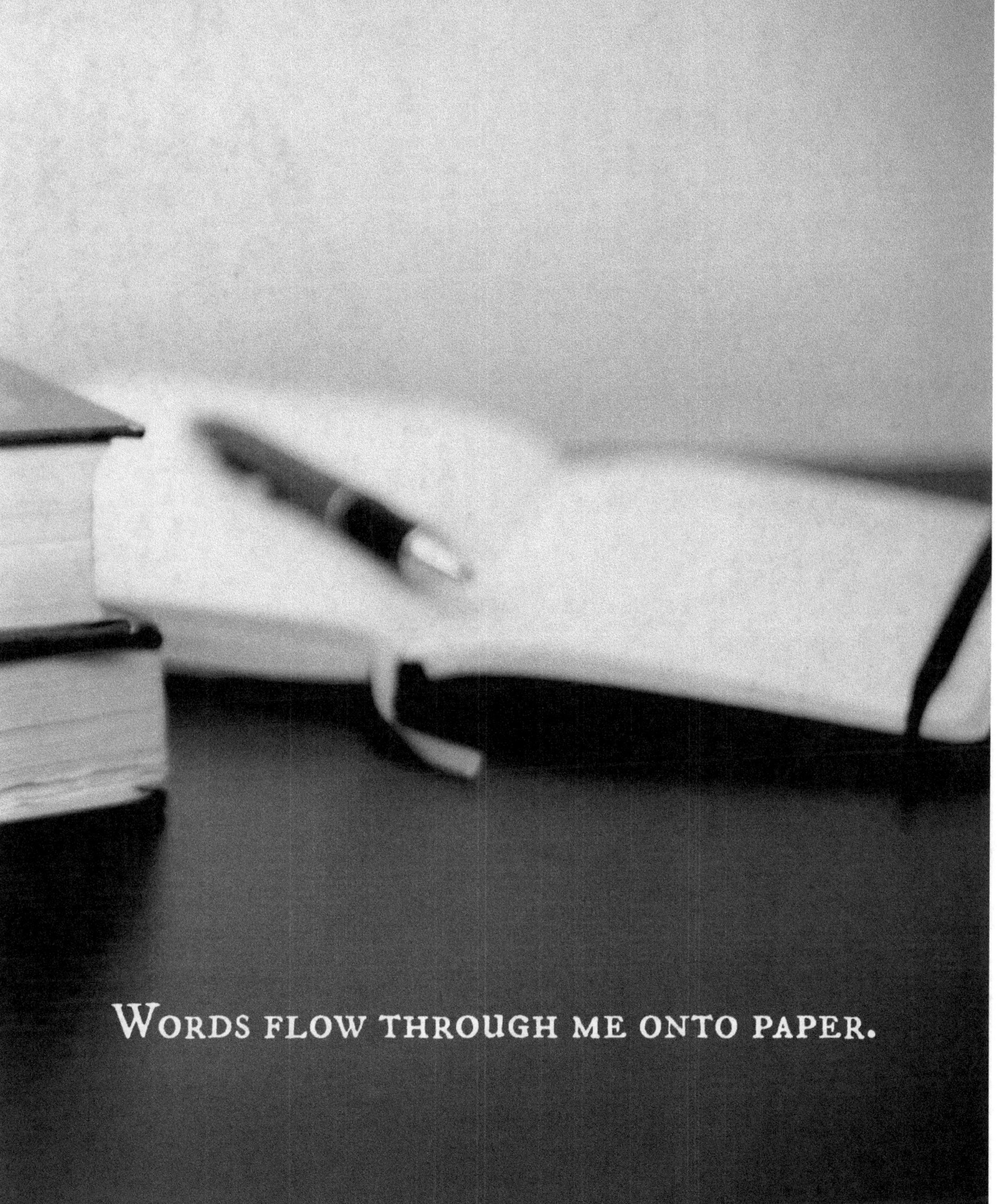

WORDS FLOW THROUGH ME ONTO PAPER.

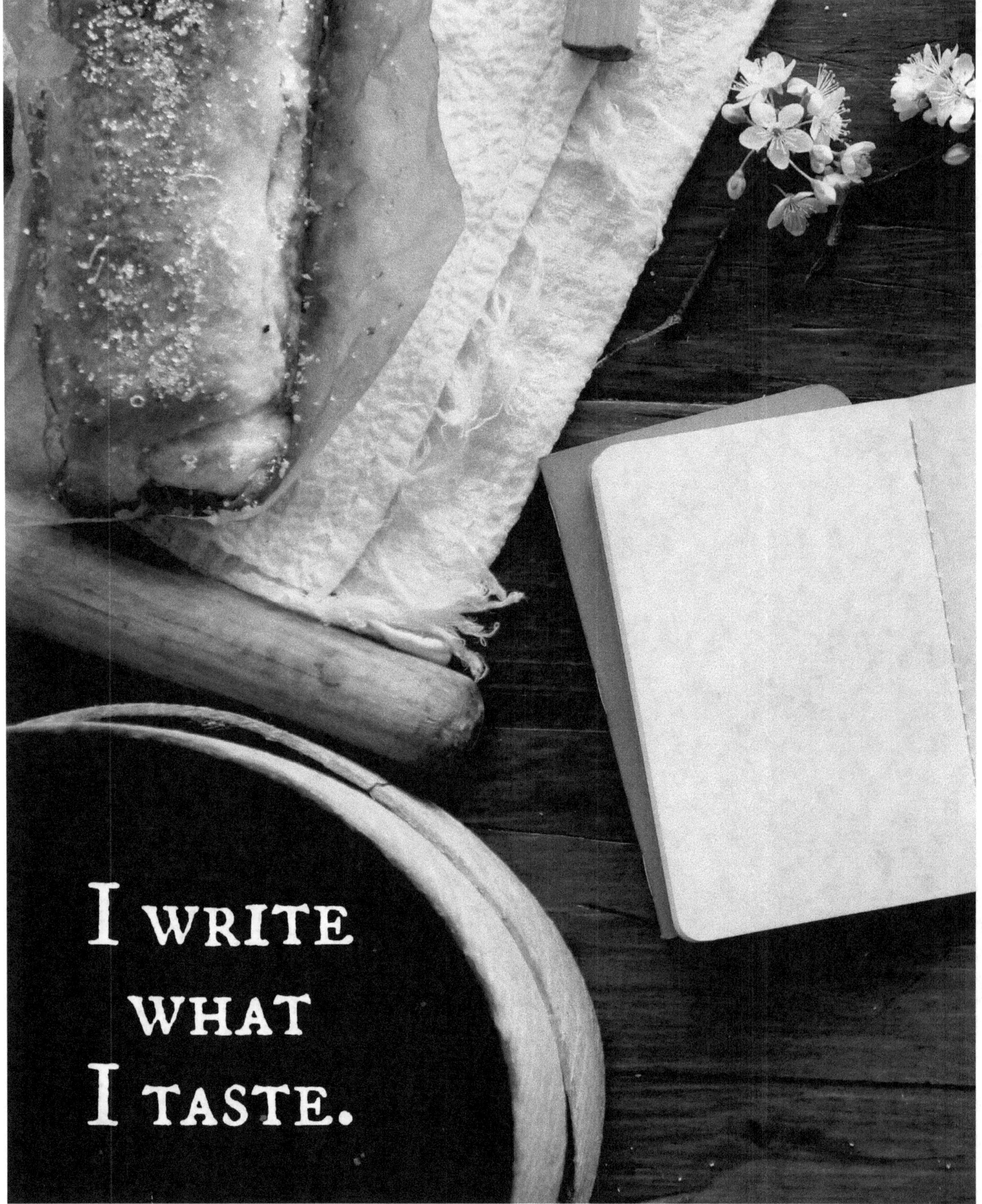

I WRITE
WHAT
I TASTE.

I NEVER STOP WRITING.

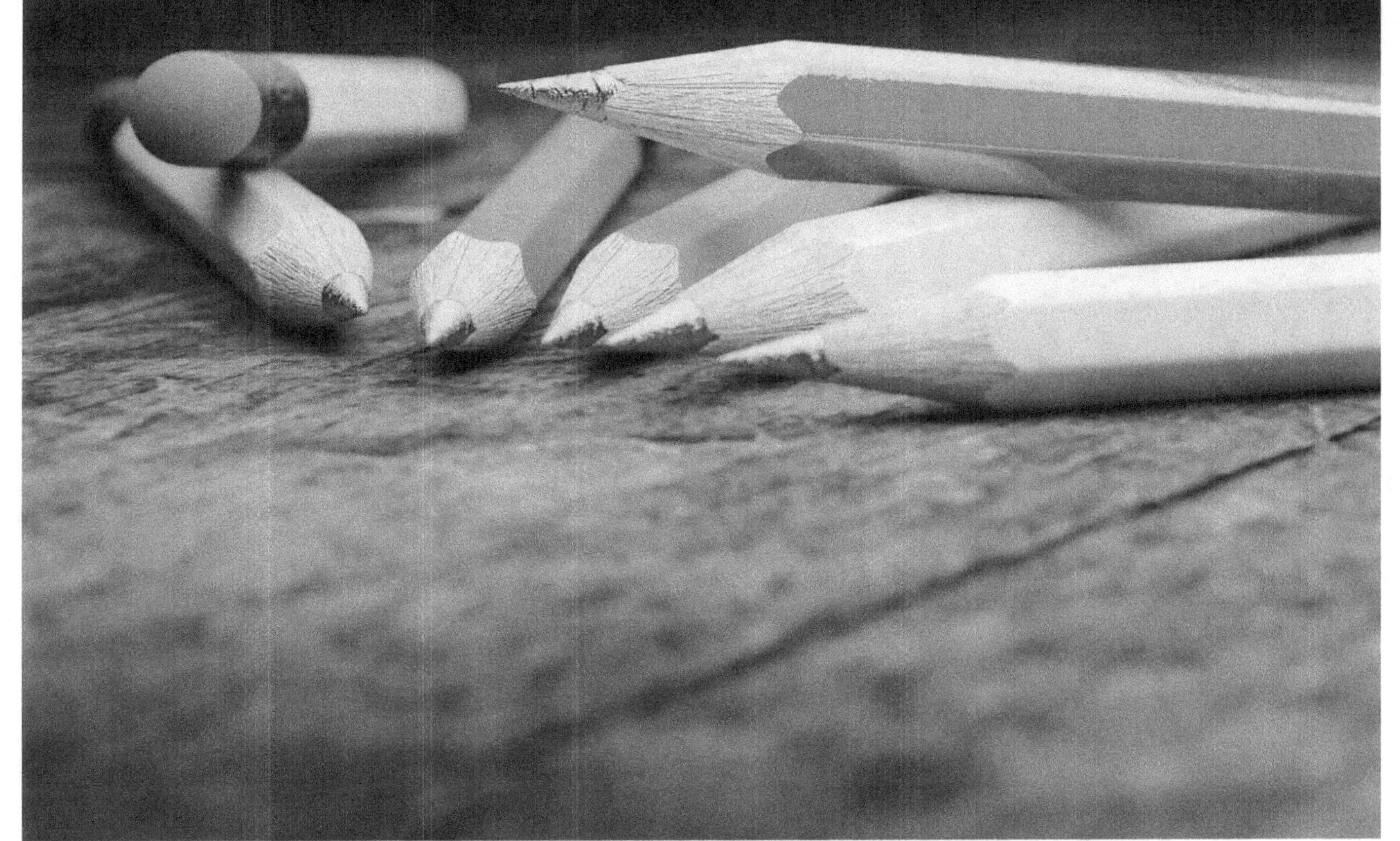

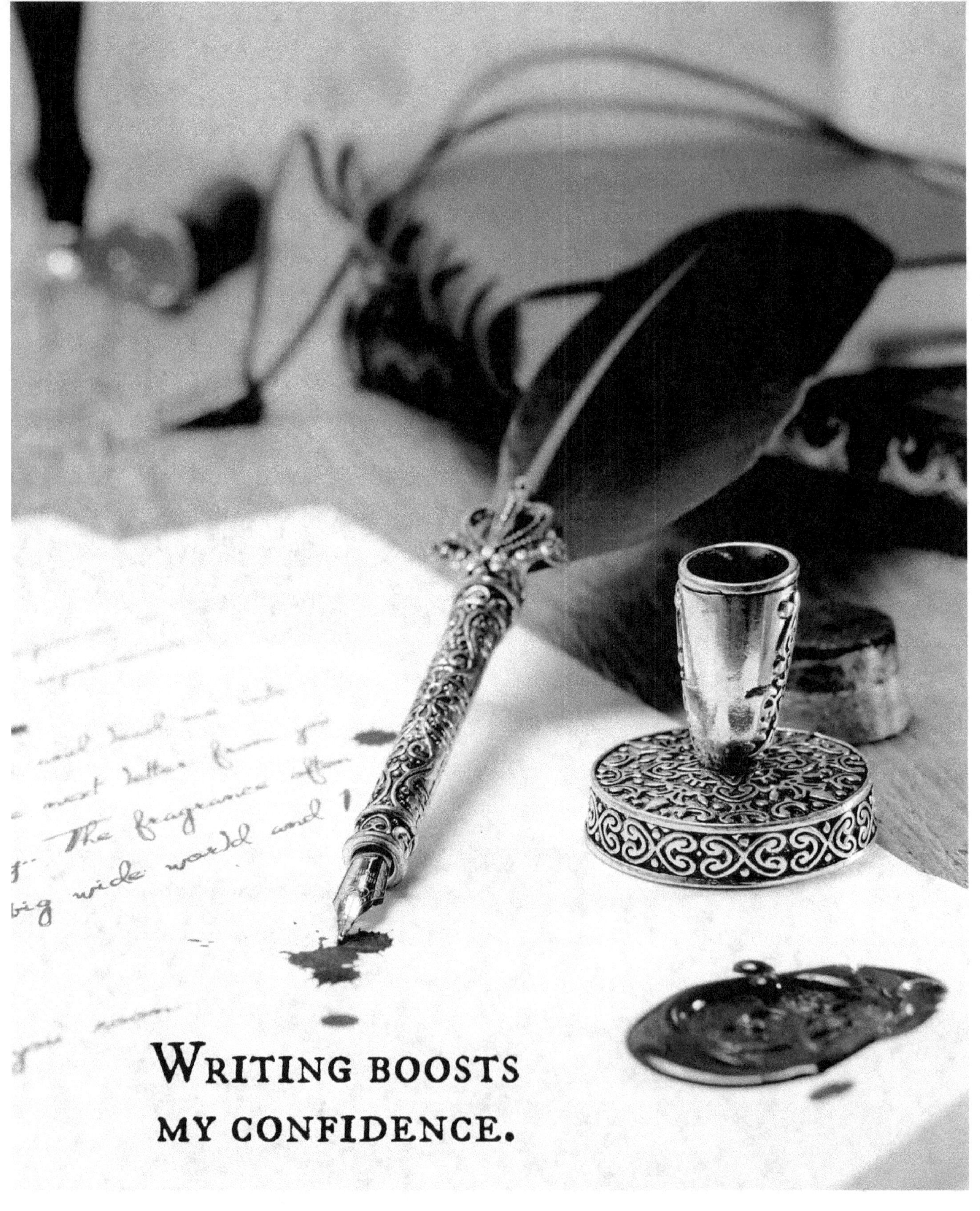
WRITING BOOSTS
MY CONFIDENCE.

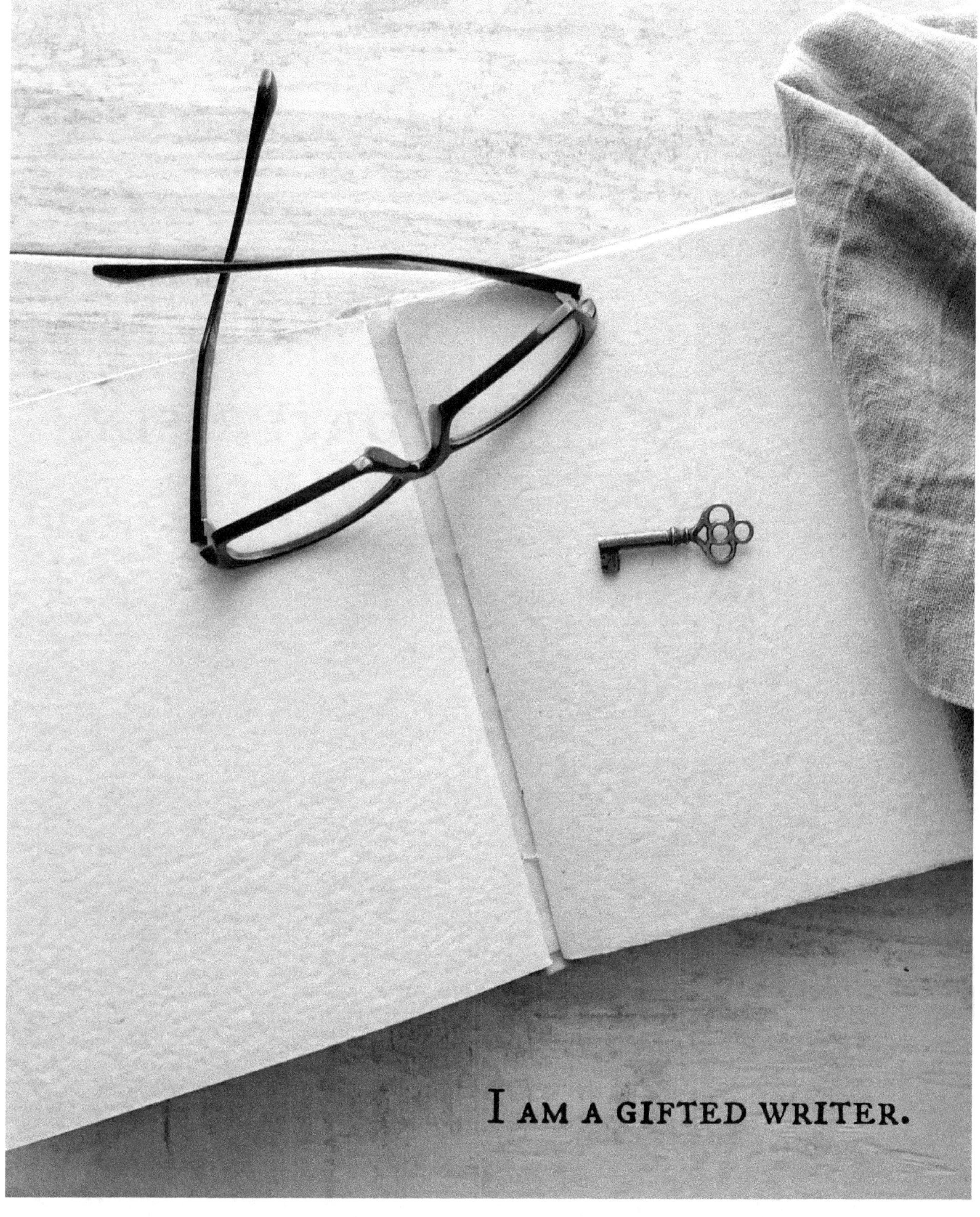
I AM A GIFTED WRITER.

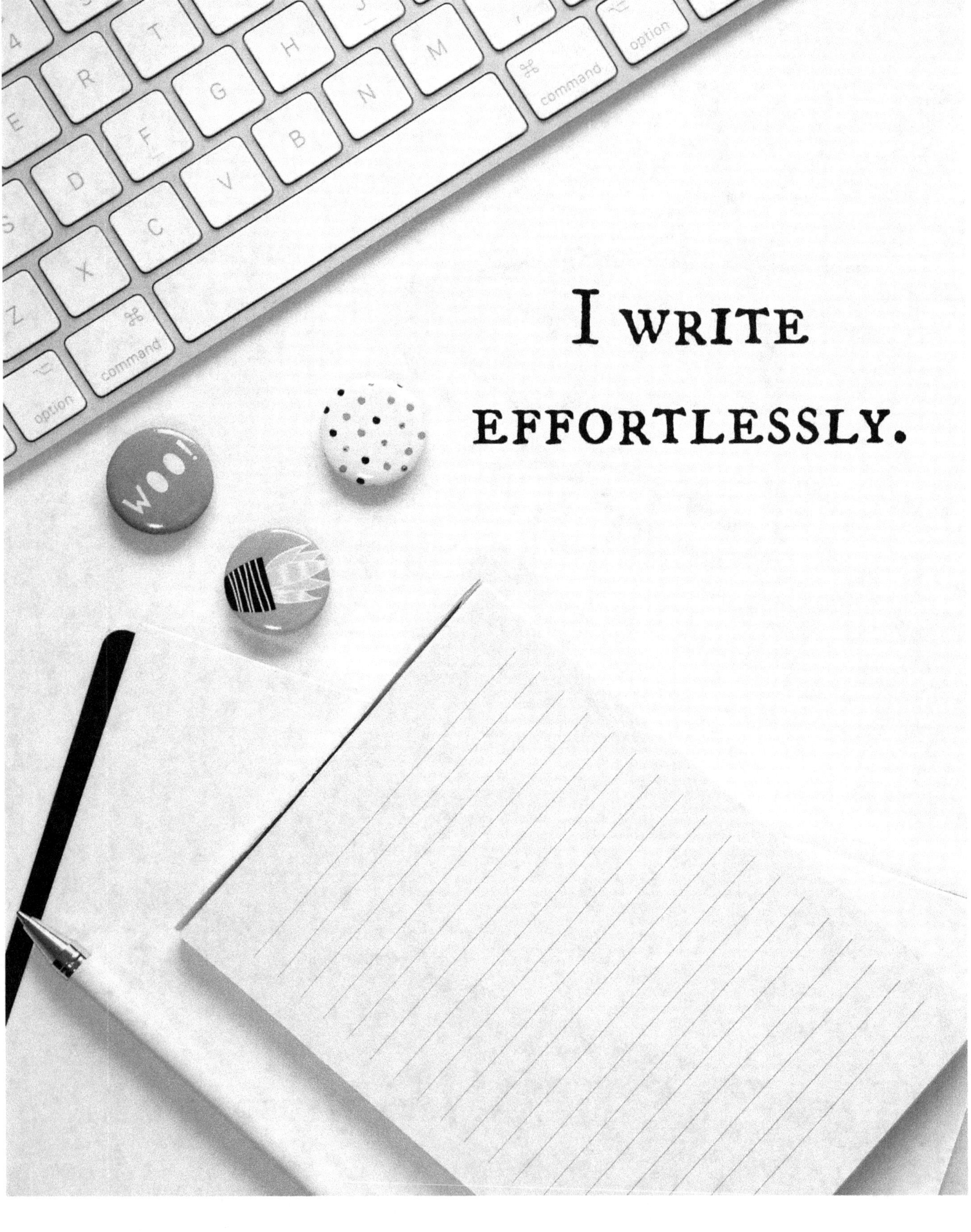

I WRITE
EFFORTLESSLY.

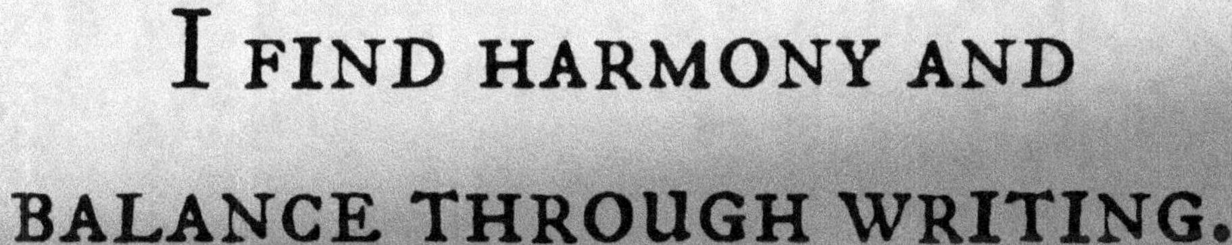

I FIND HARMONY AND
BALANCE THROUGH WRITING.

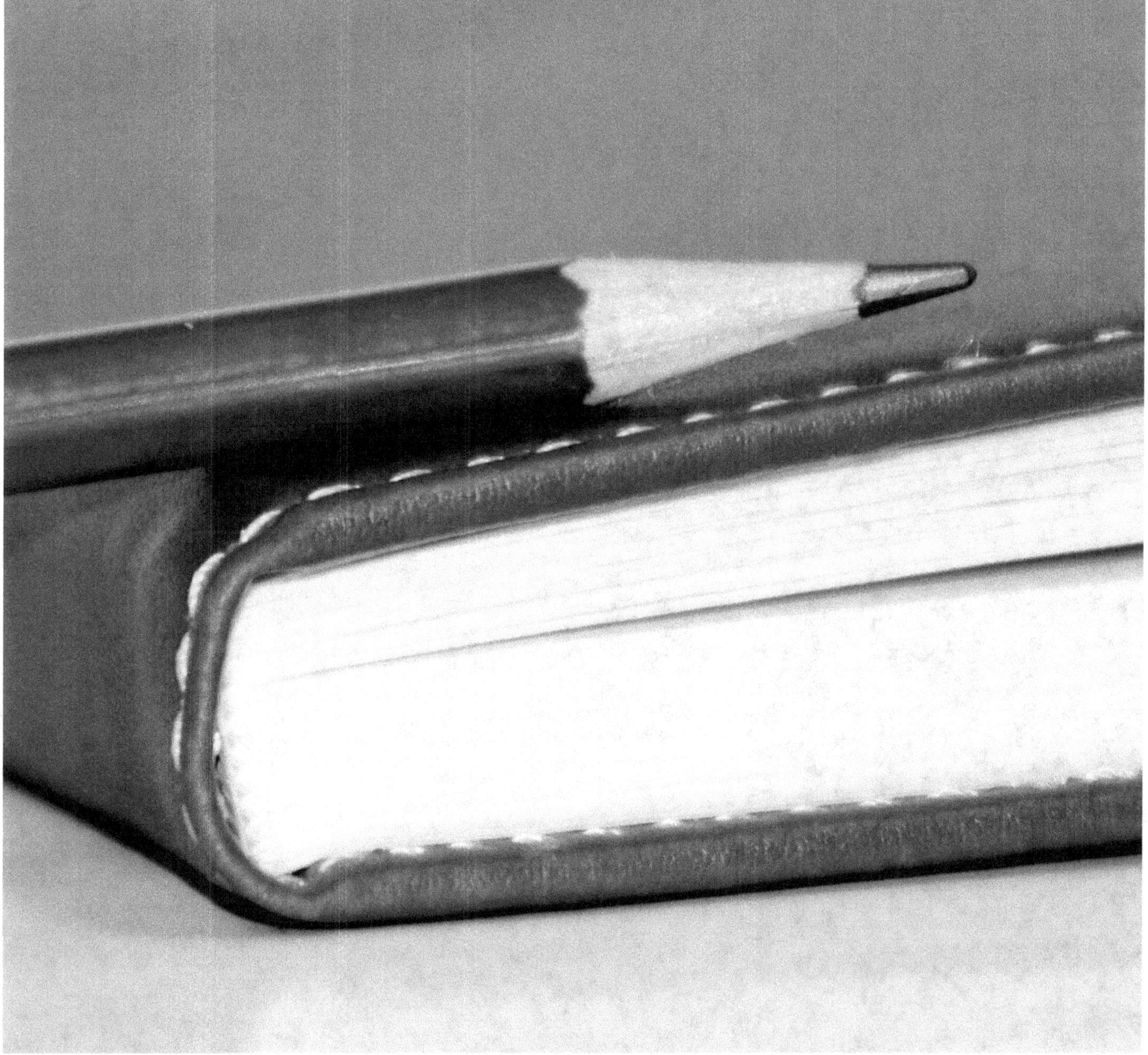

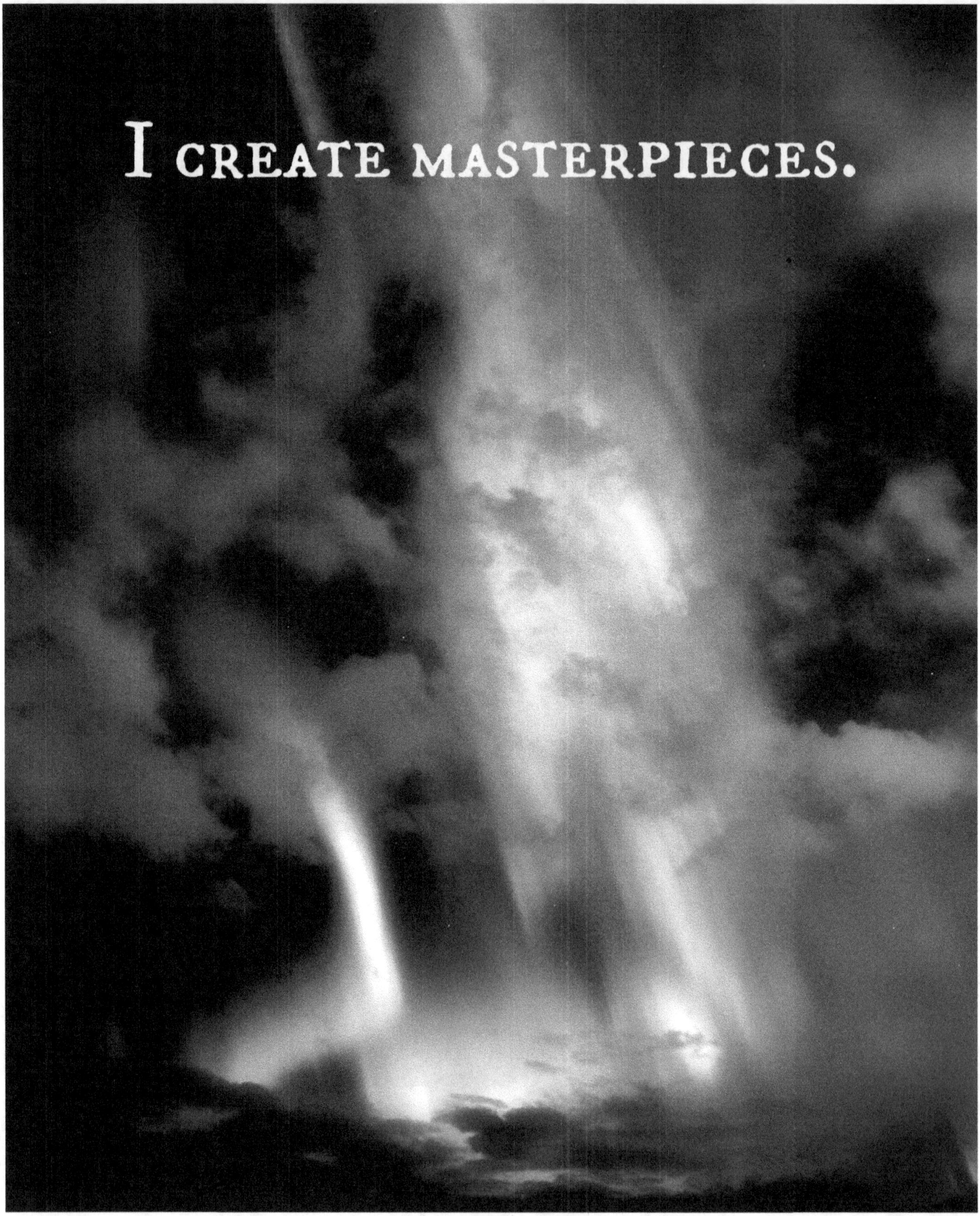

I CREATE MASTERPIECES.

I HAVE A PLETHORA OF GREAT IDEAS.

I WRITE WHAT FEELS RIGHT.

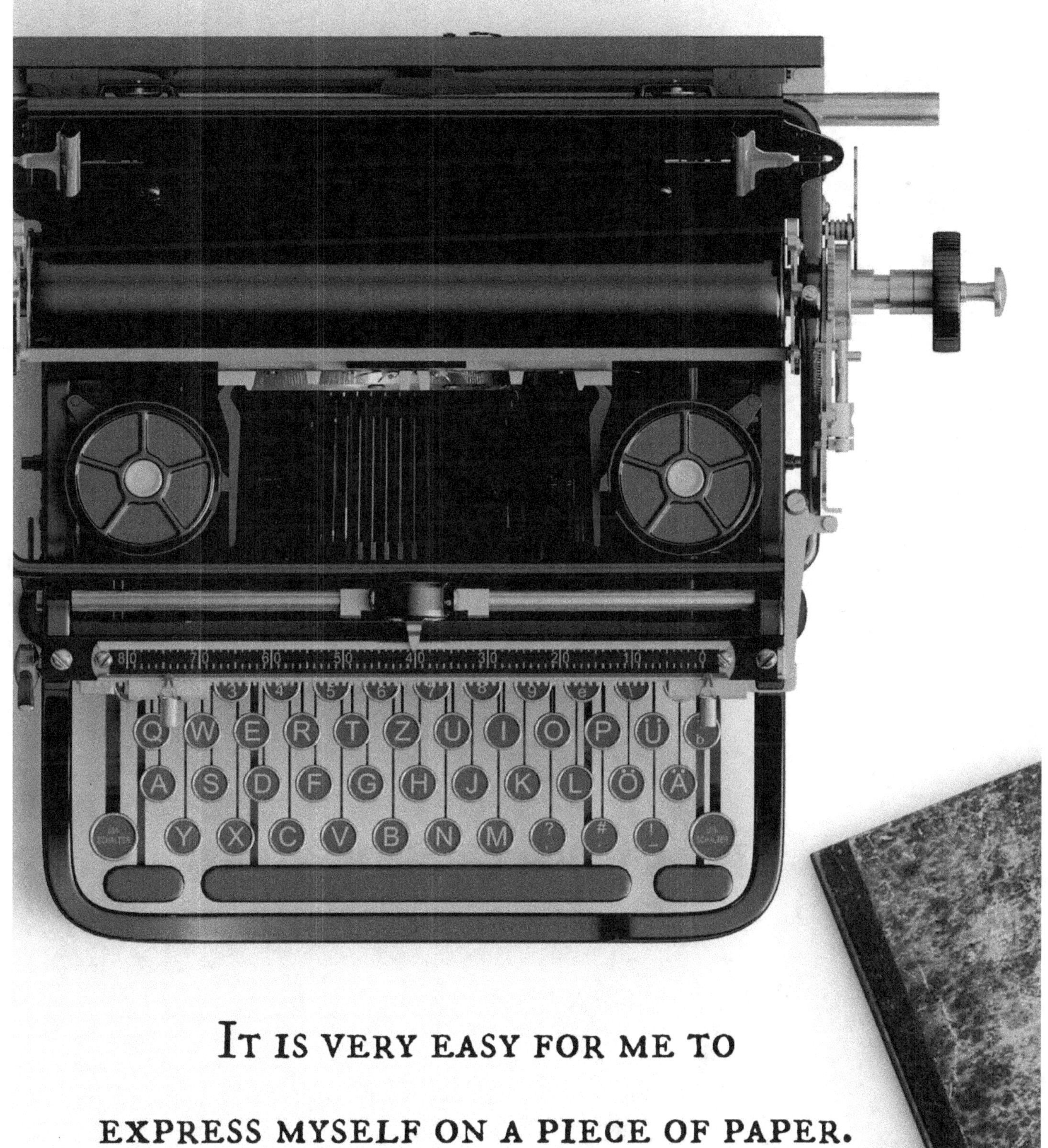

It is very easy for me to
express myself on a piece of paper.

My pen
is my
best friend.

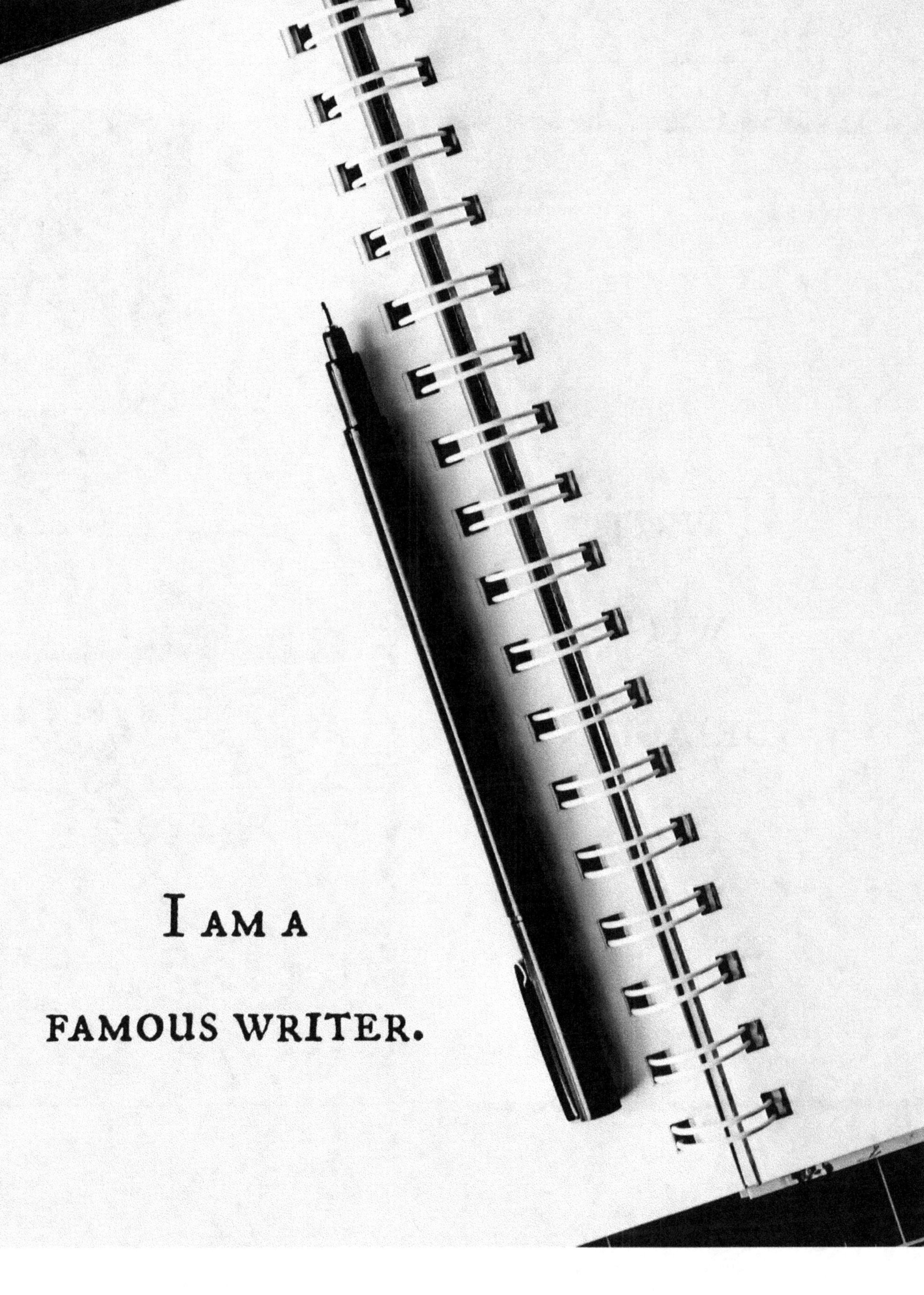

I AM A
FAMOUS WRITER.

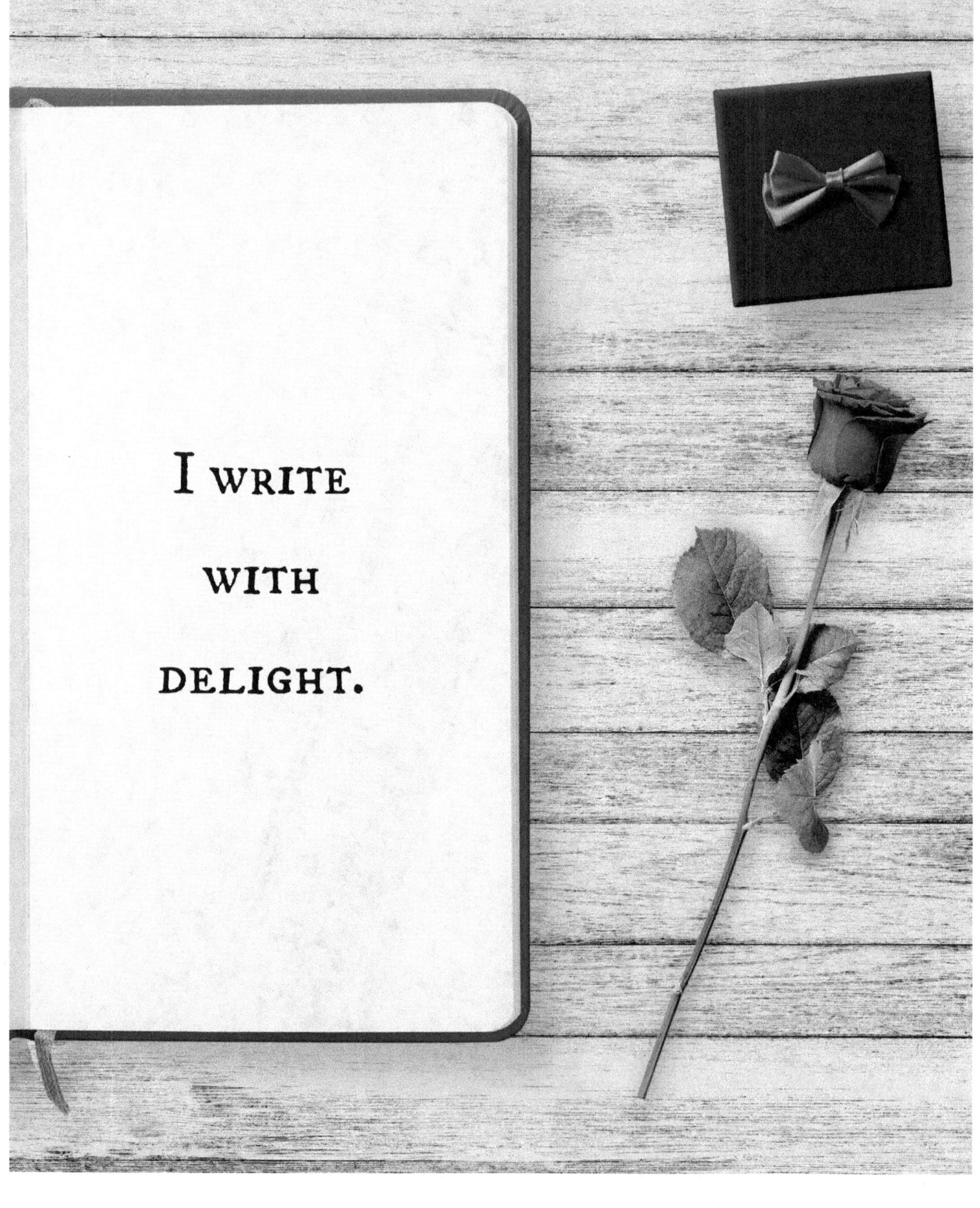

I write
with
delight.

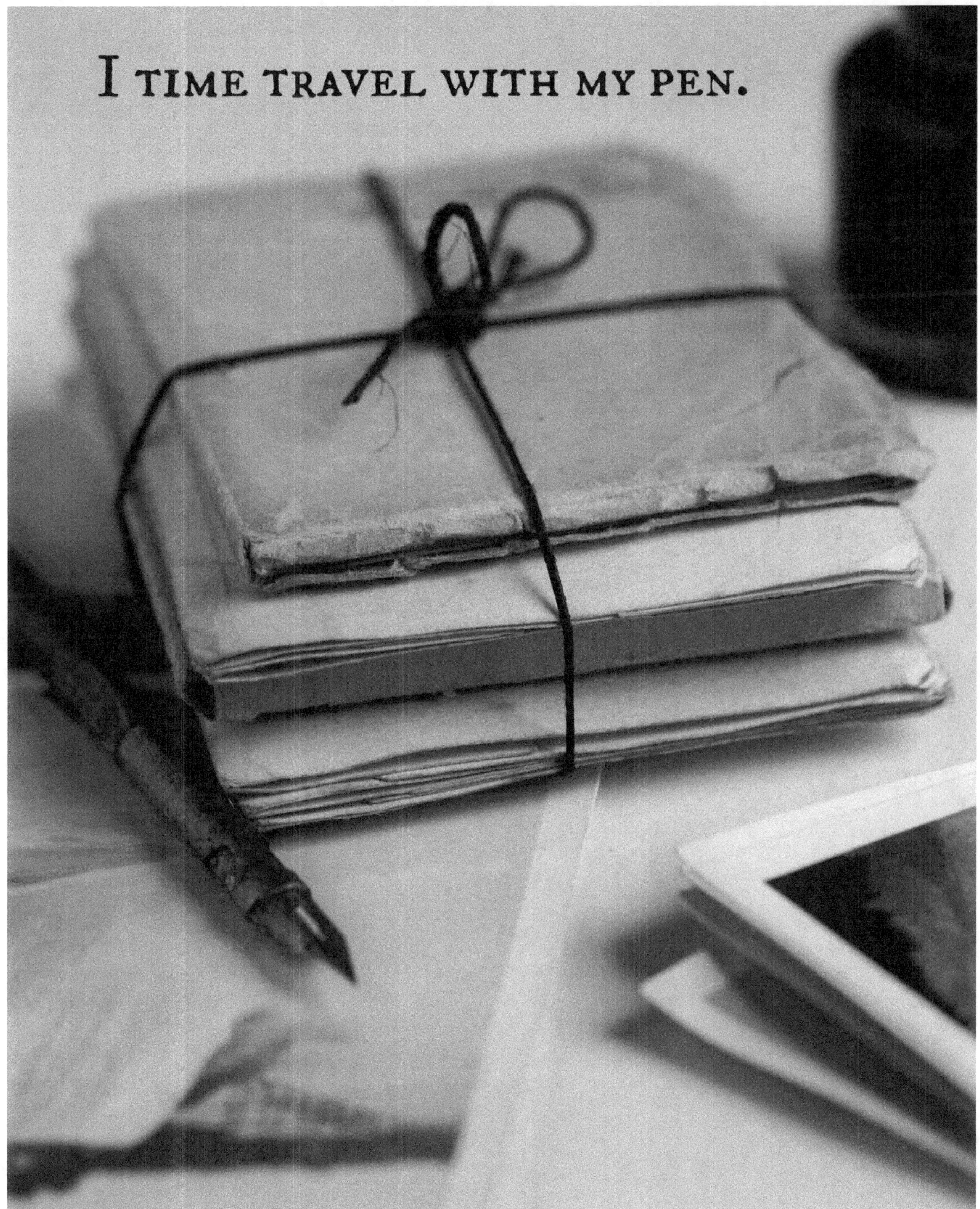

I time travel with my pen.

WRITING HEALS ME.

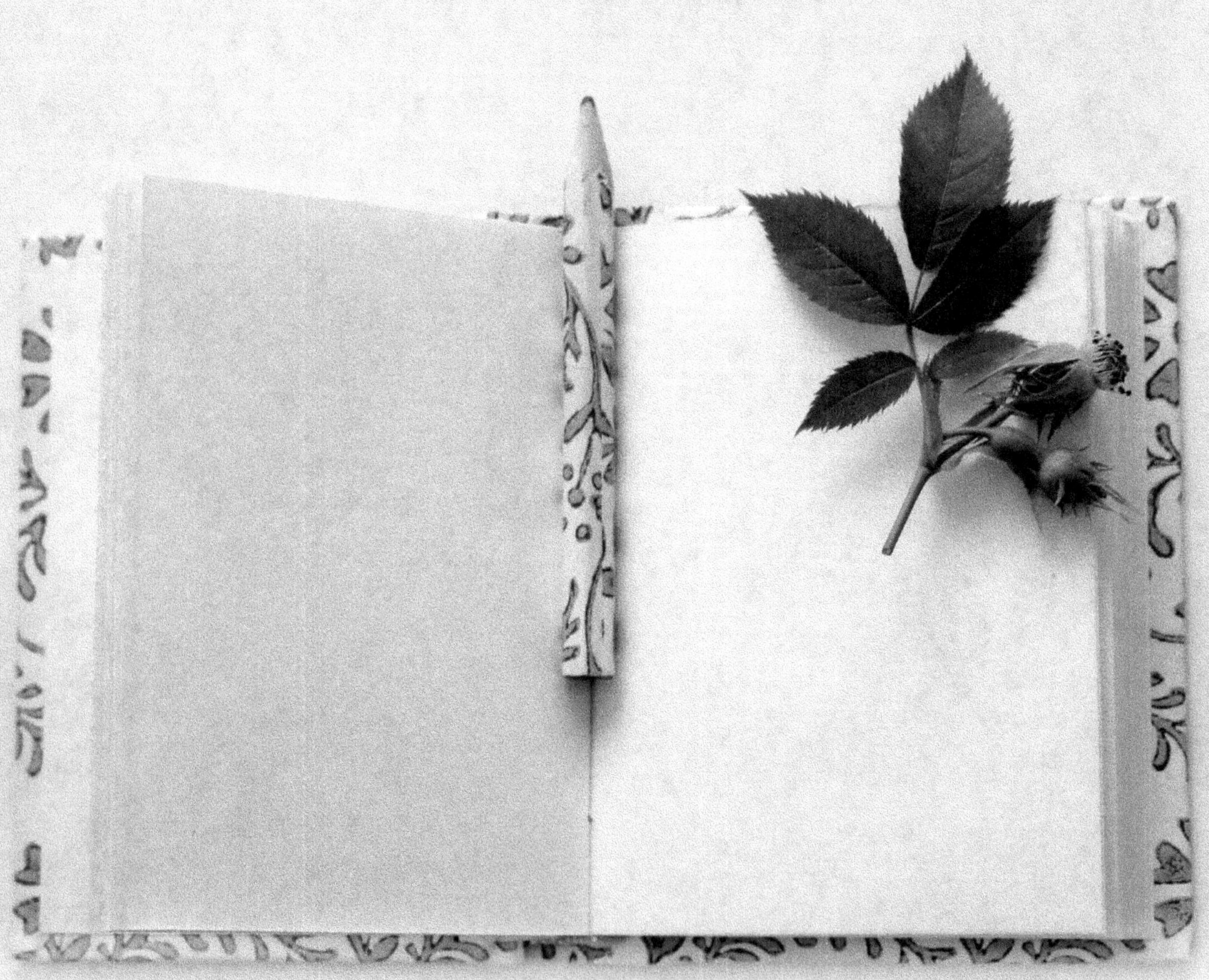

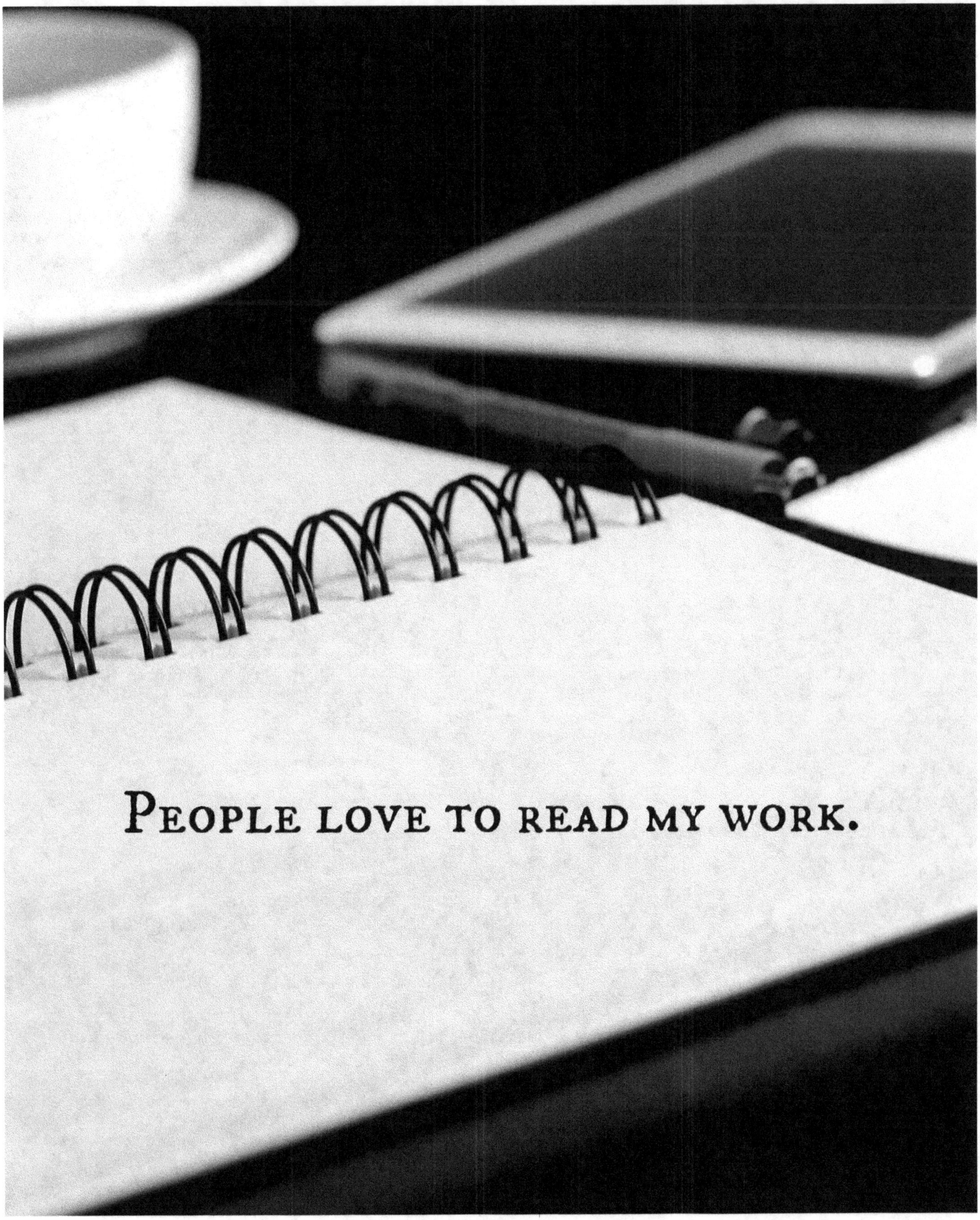

PEOPLE LOVE TO READ MY WORK.

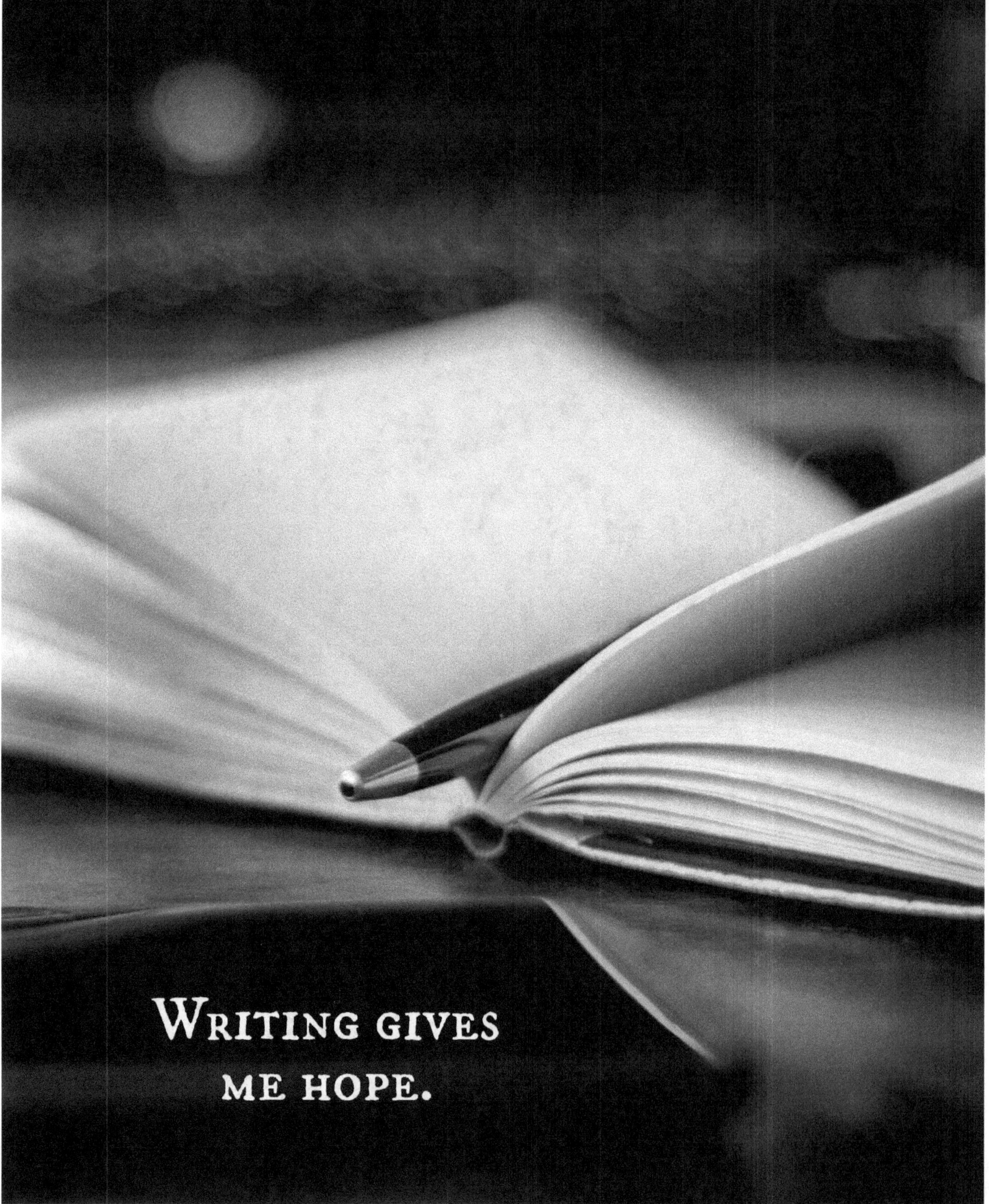
WRITING GIVES
ME HOPE.

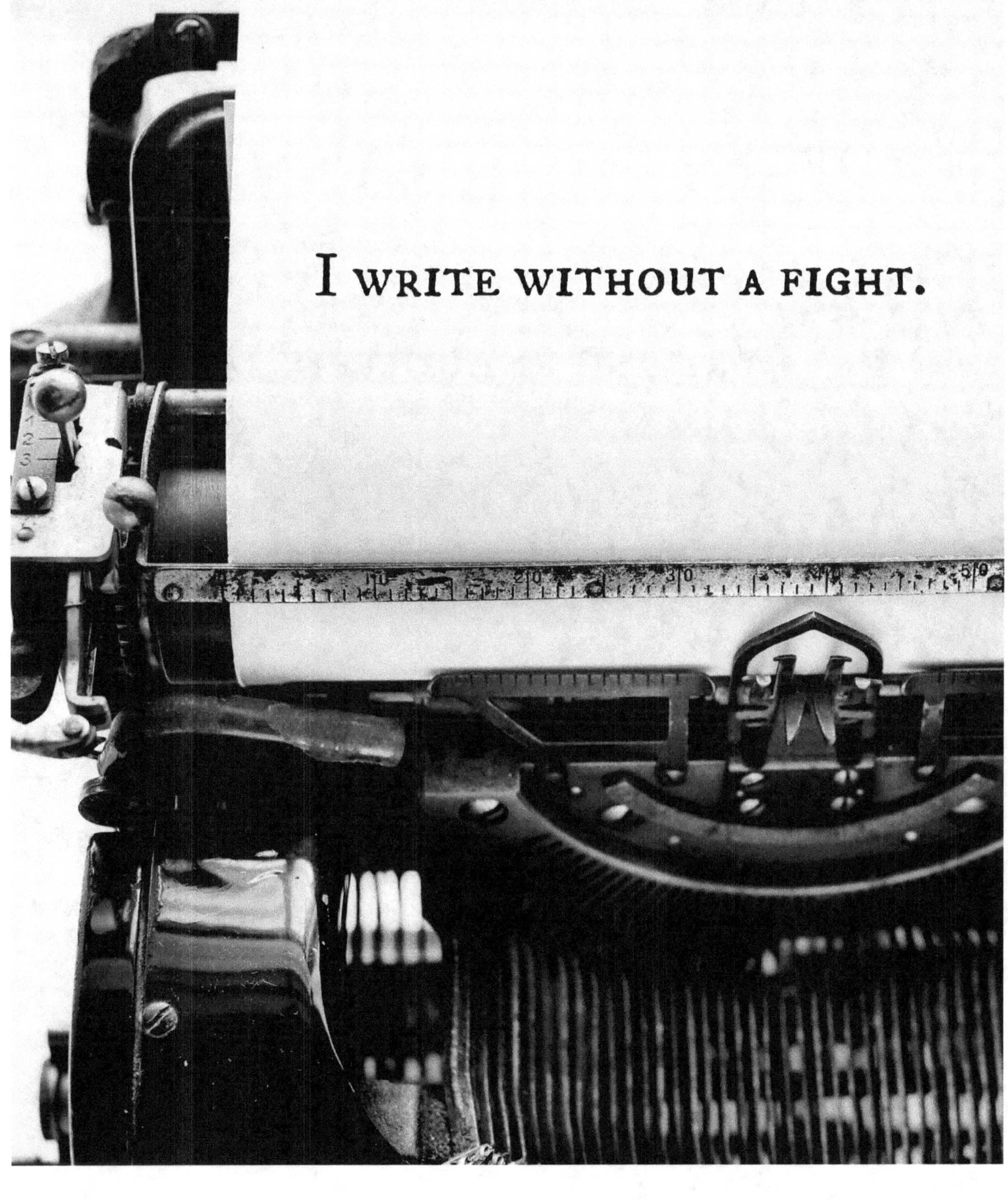
I WRITE WITHOUT A FIGHT.

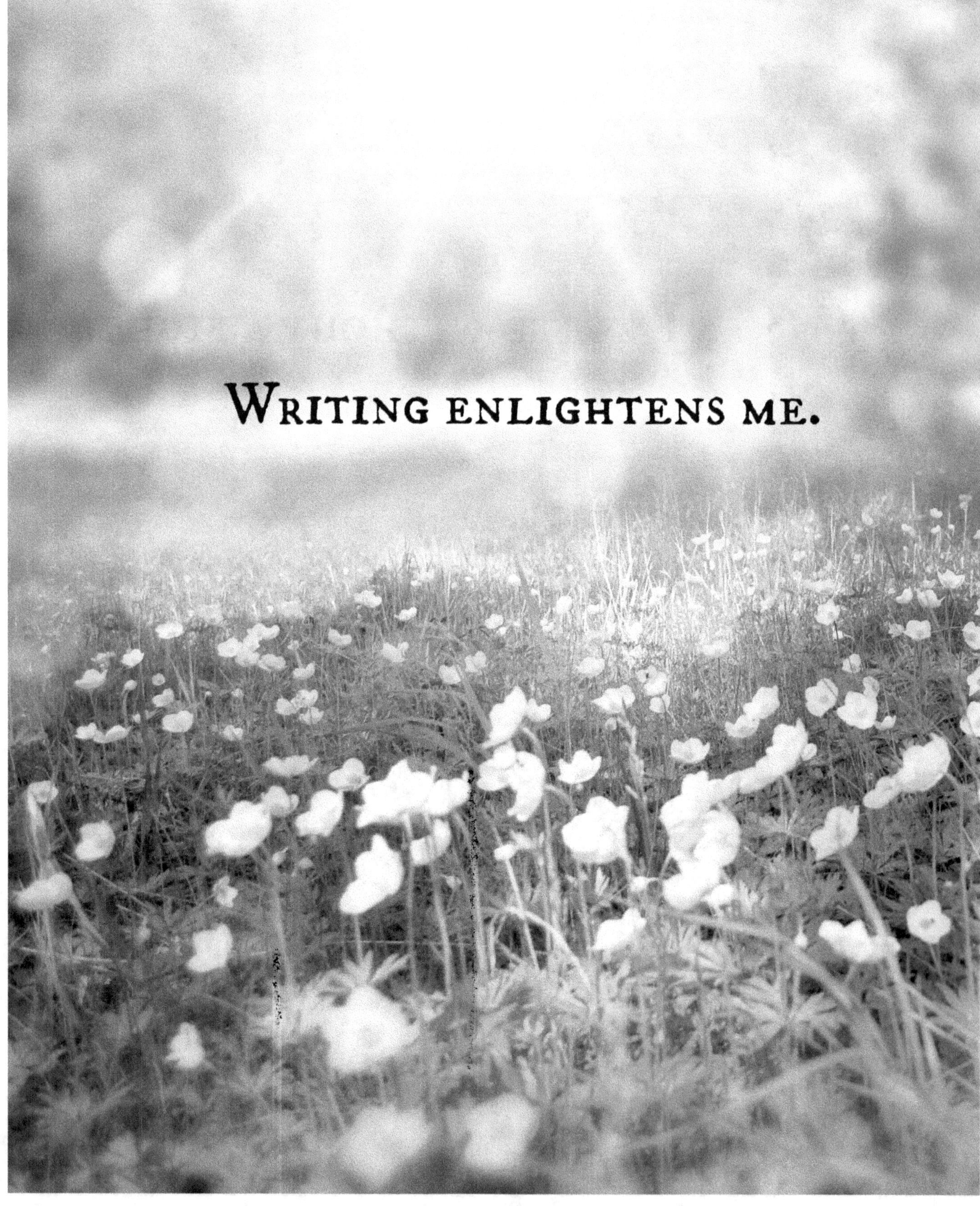
WRITING ENLIGHTENS ME.

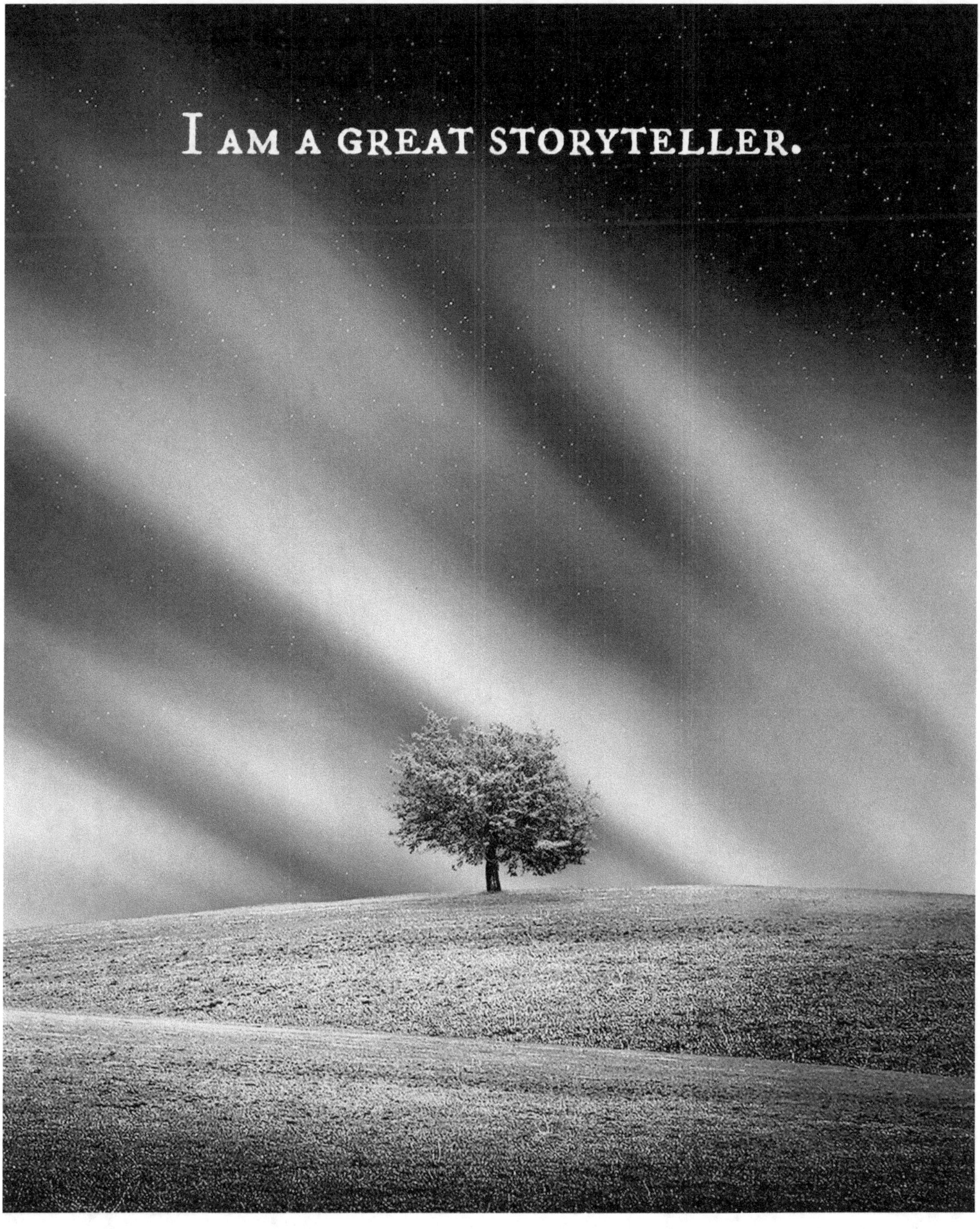

I AM A GREAT STORYTELLER.

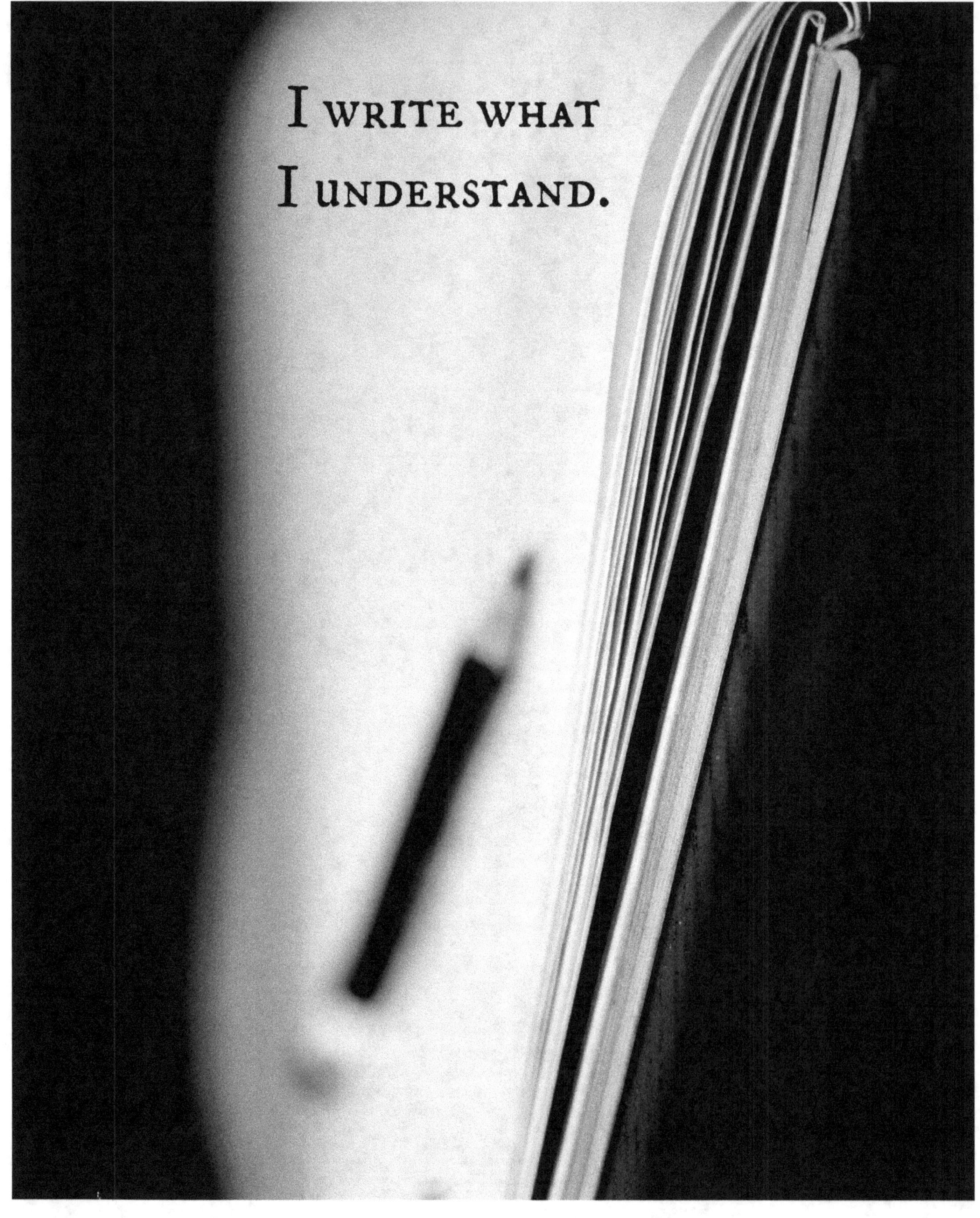

I write what
I understand.

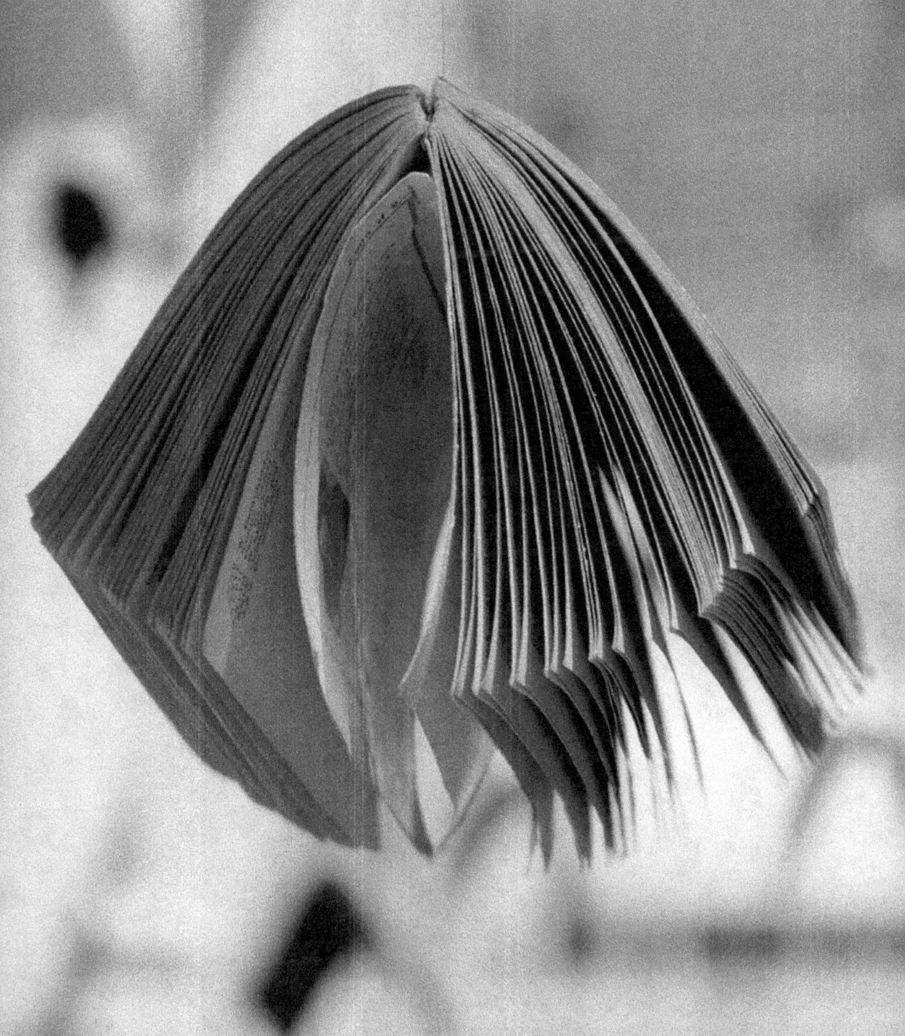

WRITING KEEPS ME YOUNG.

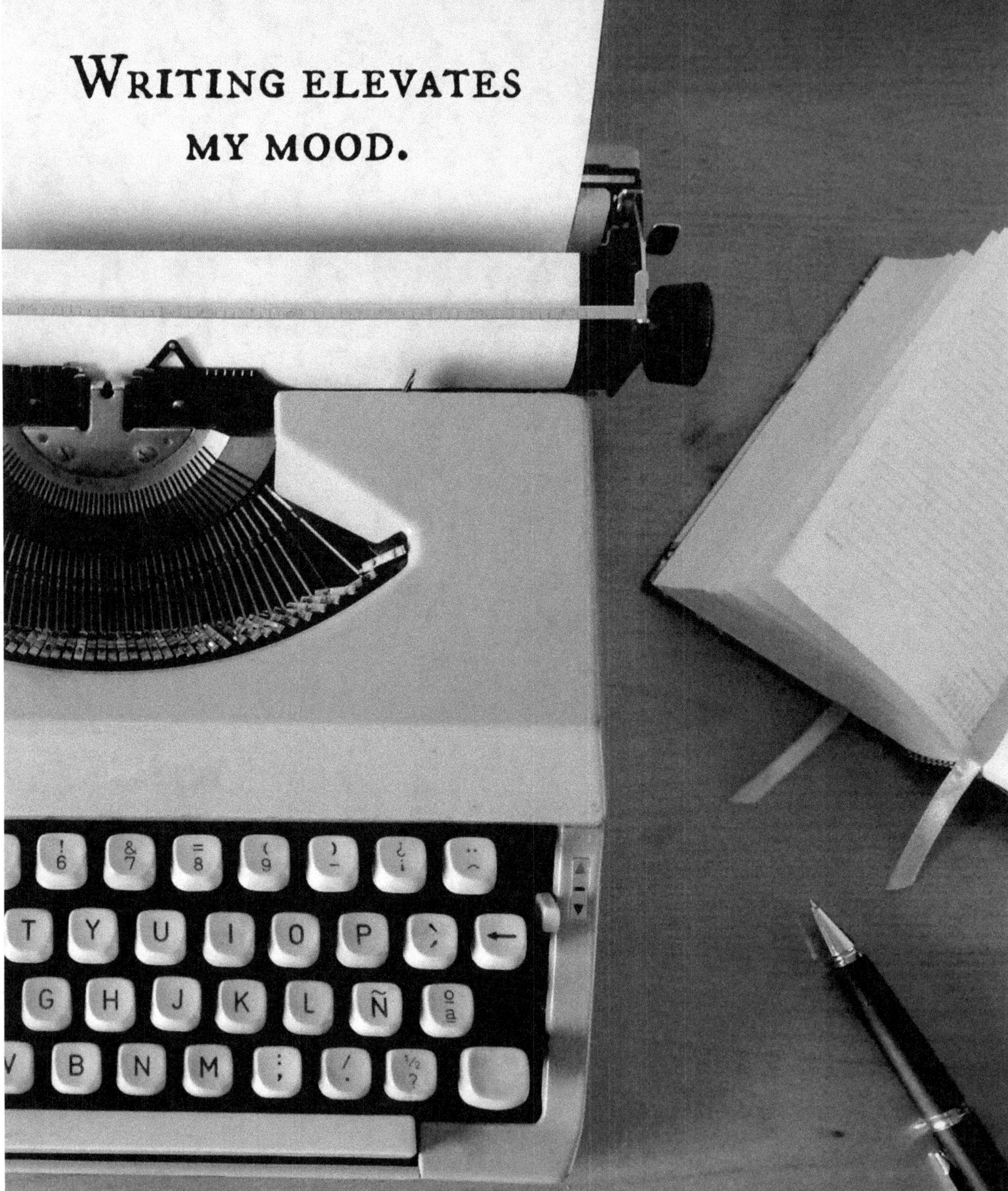
WRITING ELEVATES
MY MOOD.

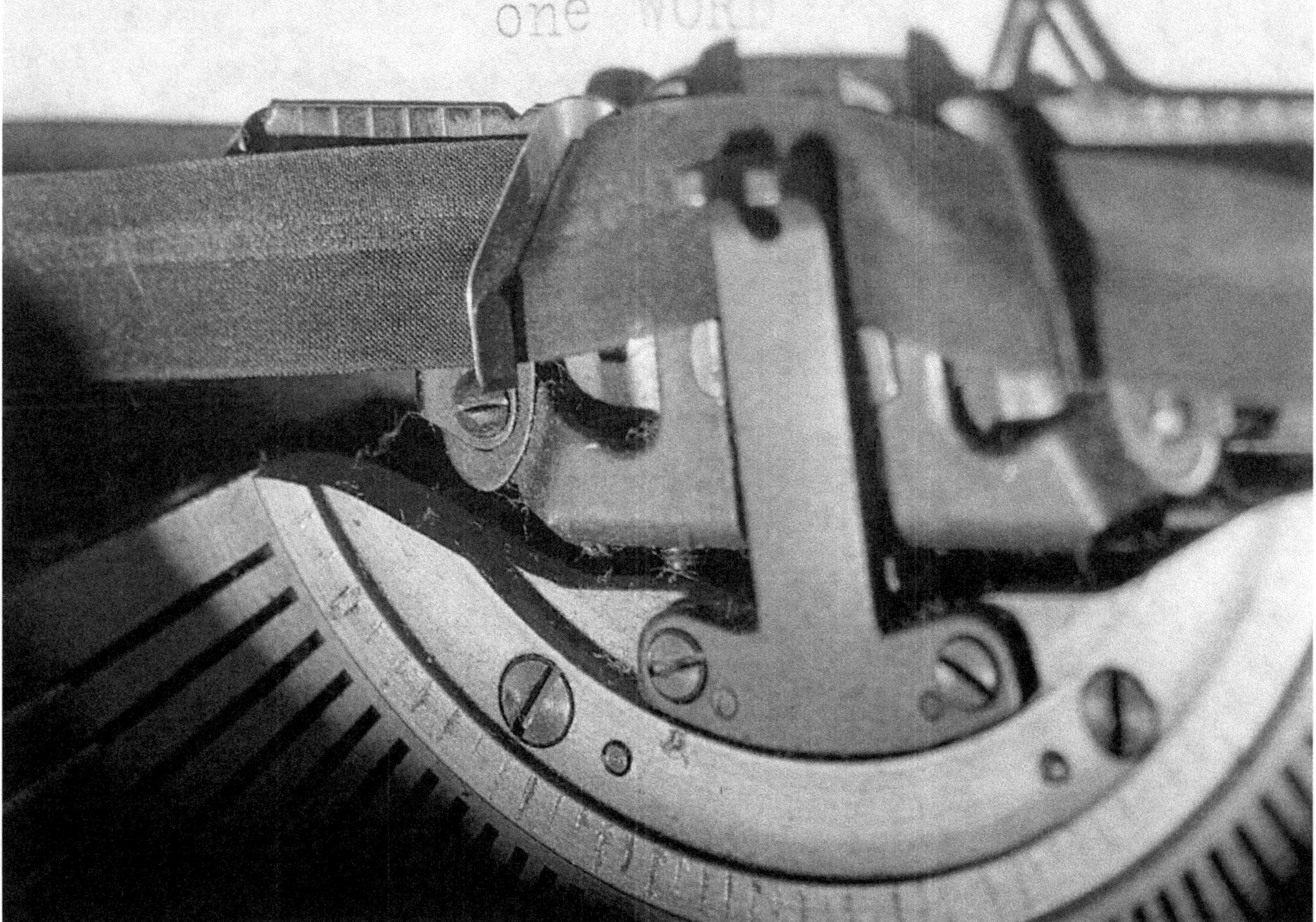
MY WORDS LEAVE A LASTING IMPRESSION.
It starts with one WORD

I AM A HIGHLY RECOGNIZED AUTHOR.

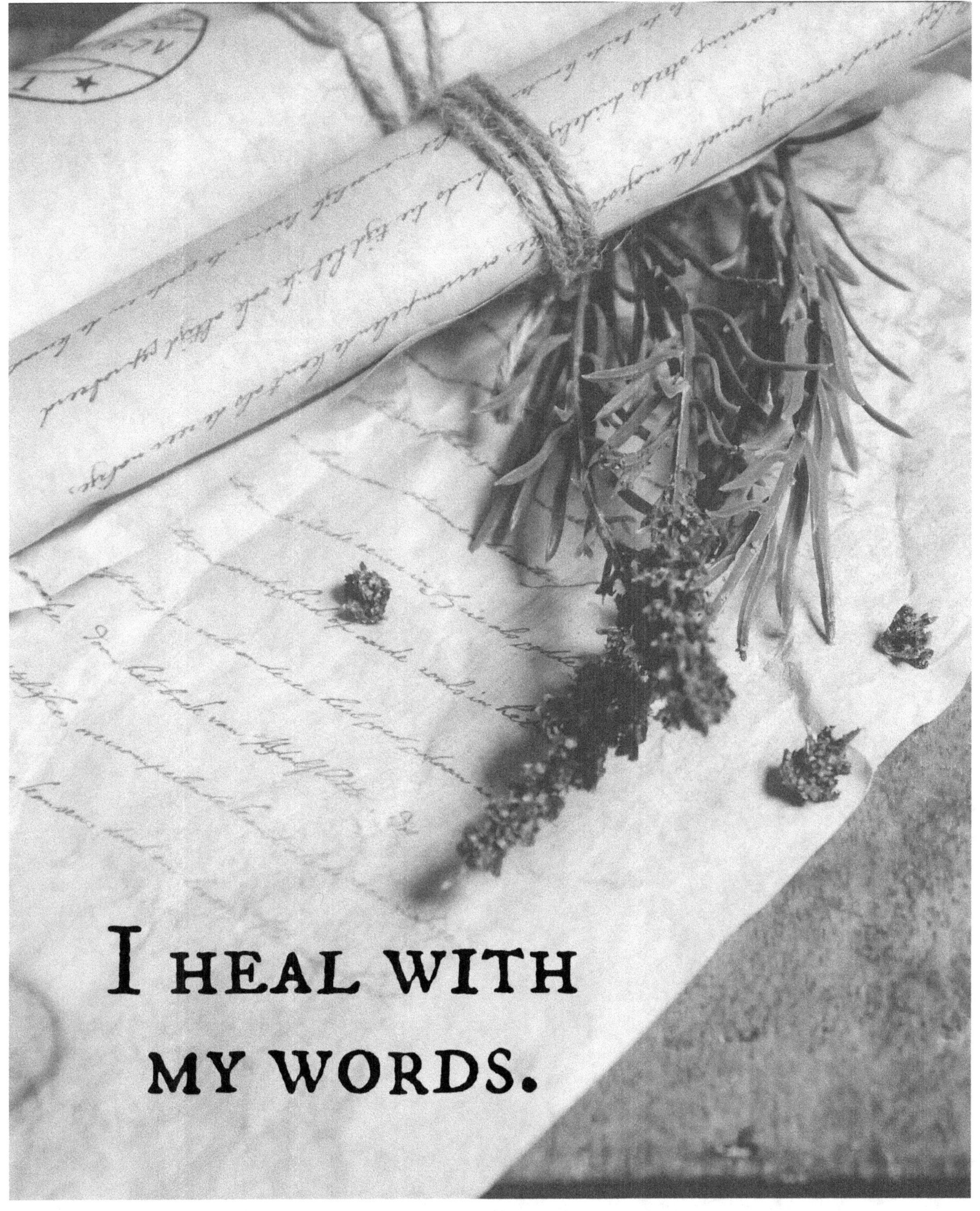

I heal with my words.

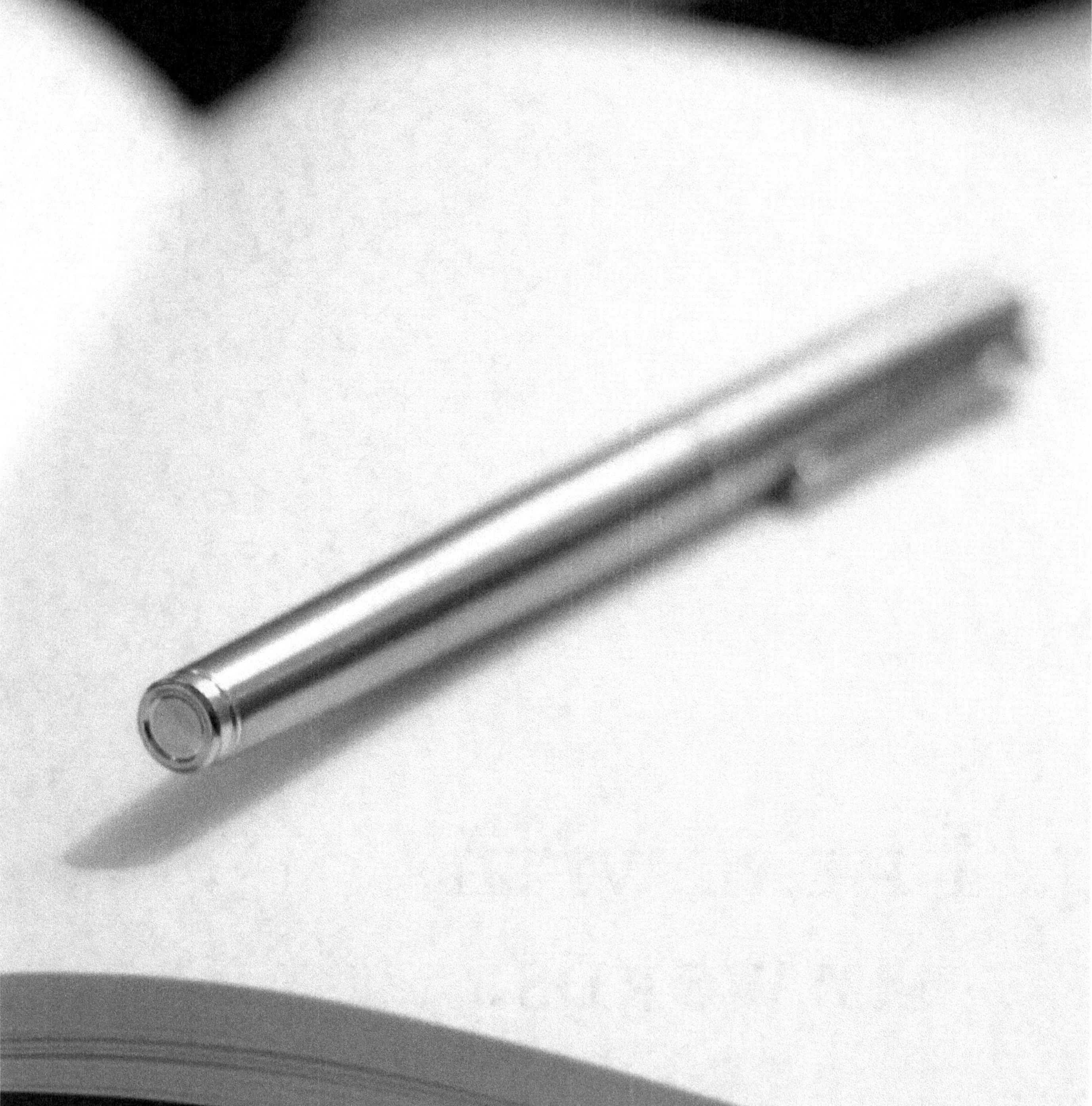

IT'S EASY FOR ME TO WRITE.

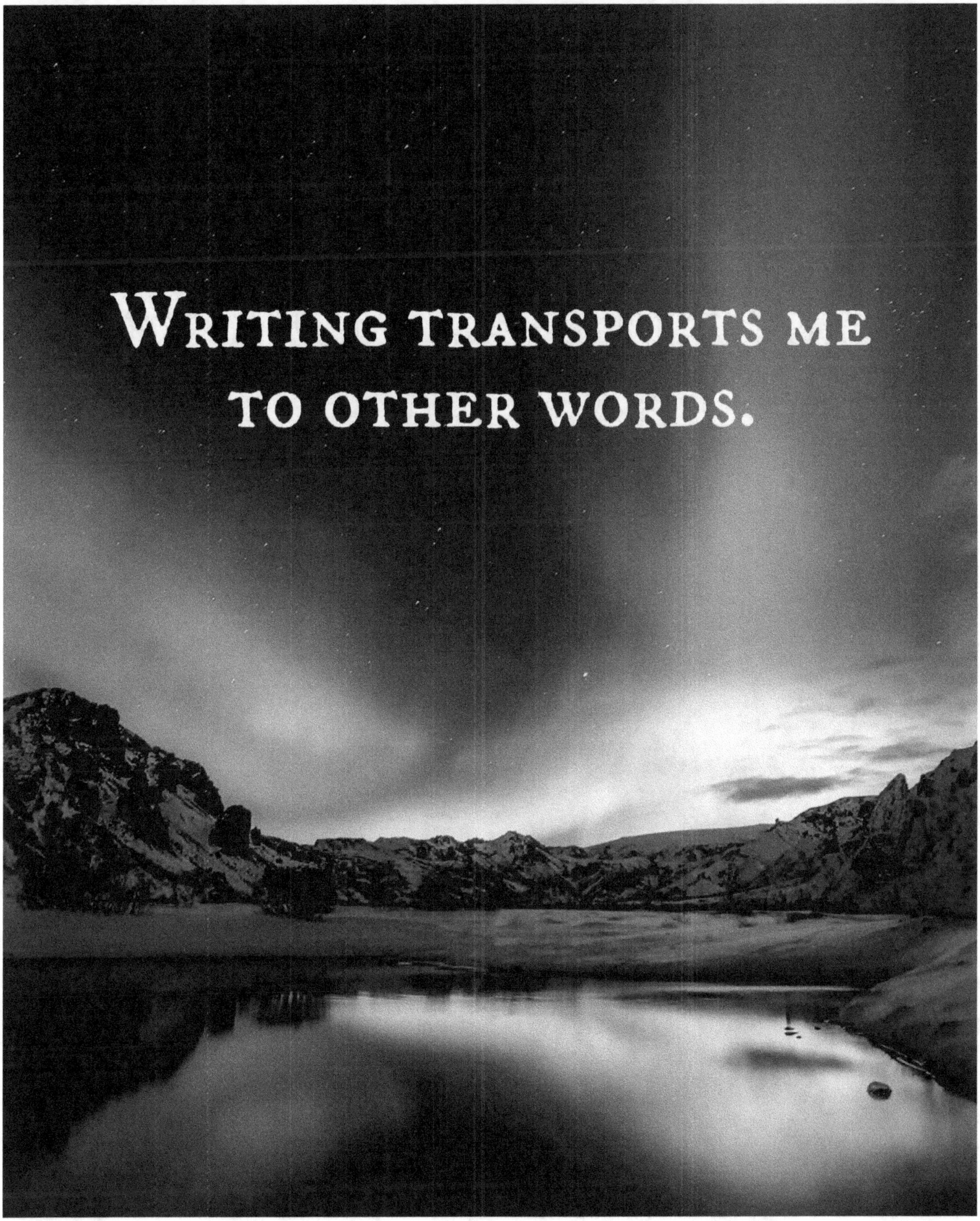

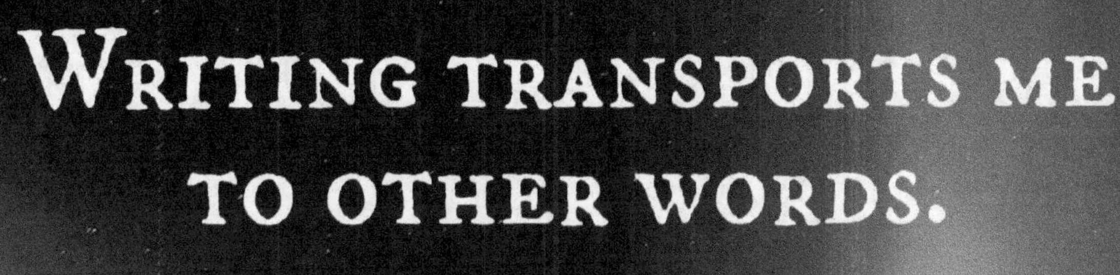

WRITING TRANSPORTS ME
TO OTHER WORDS.

I WRITE WHAT I SEE.

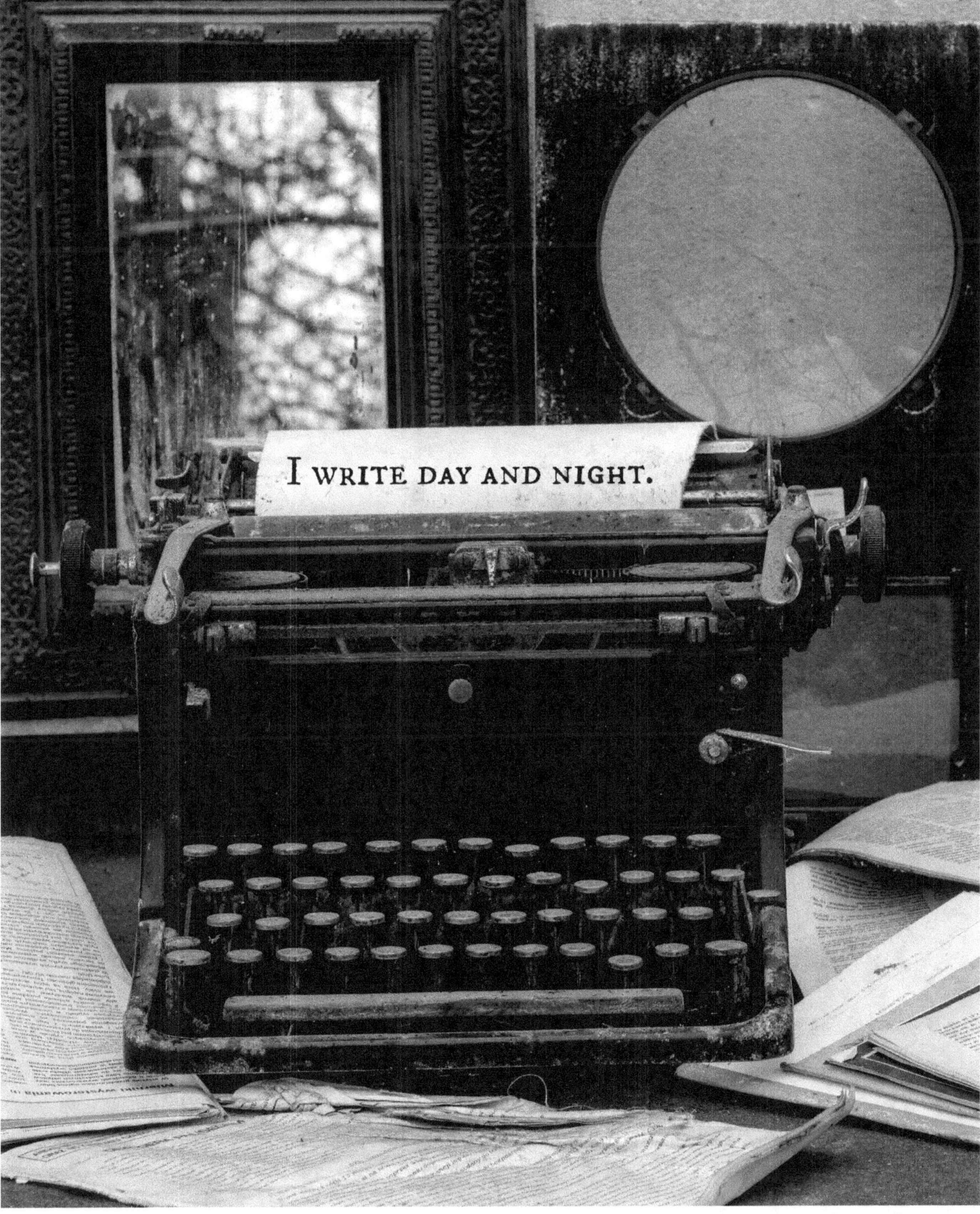
I WRITE DAY AND NIGHT.

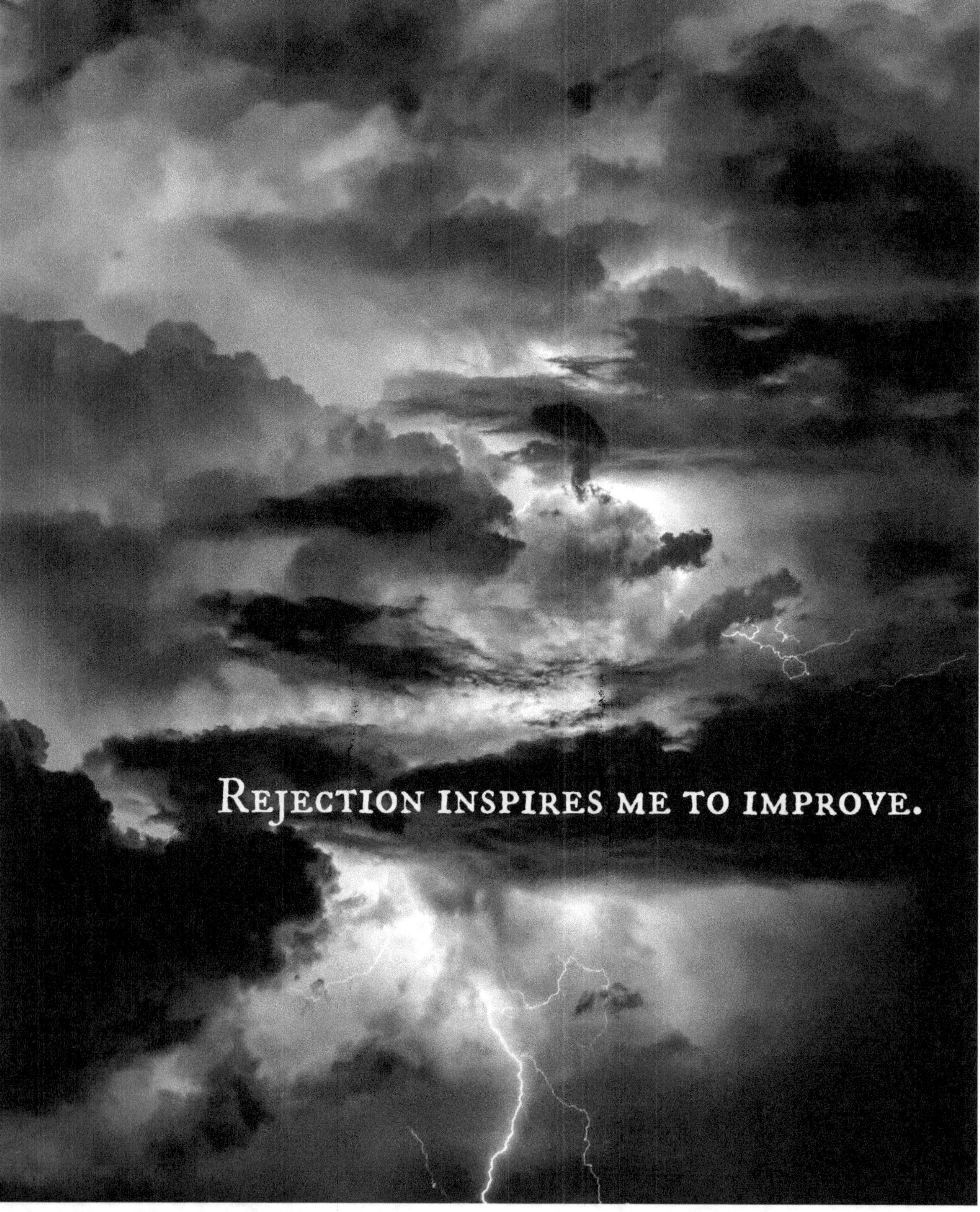REJECTION INSPIRES ME TO IMPROVE.

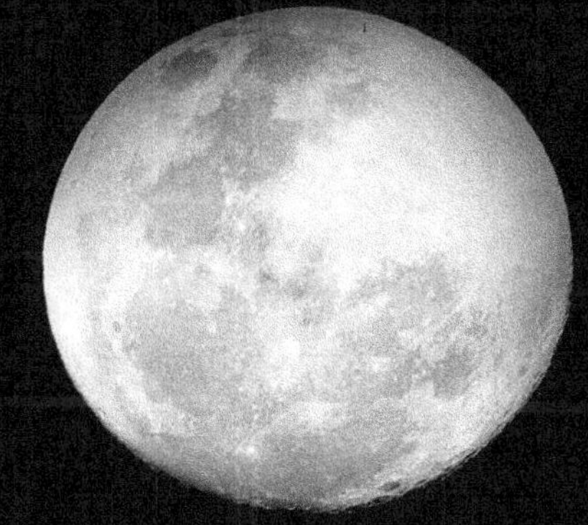

I WRITE WHAT I DREAM.

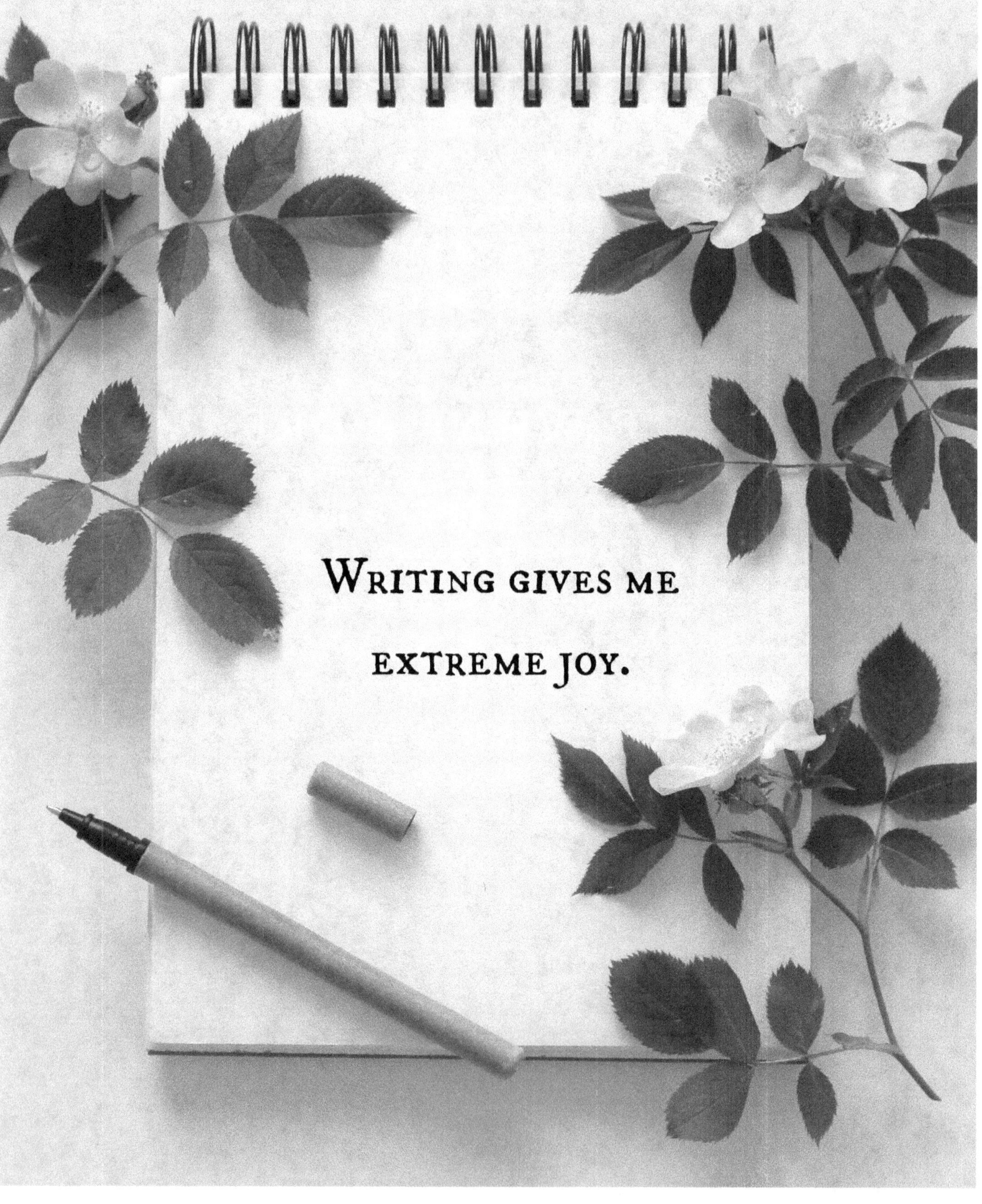

WRITING GIVES ME
EXTREME JOY.

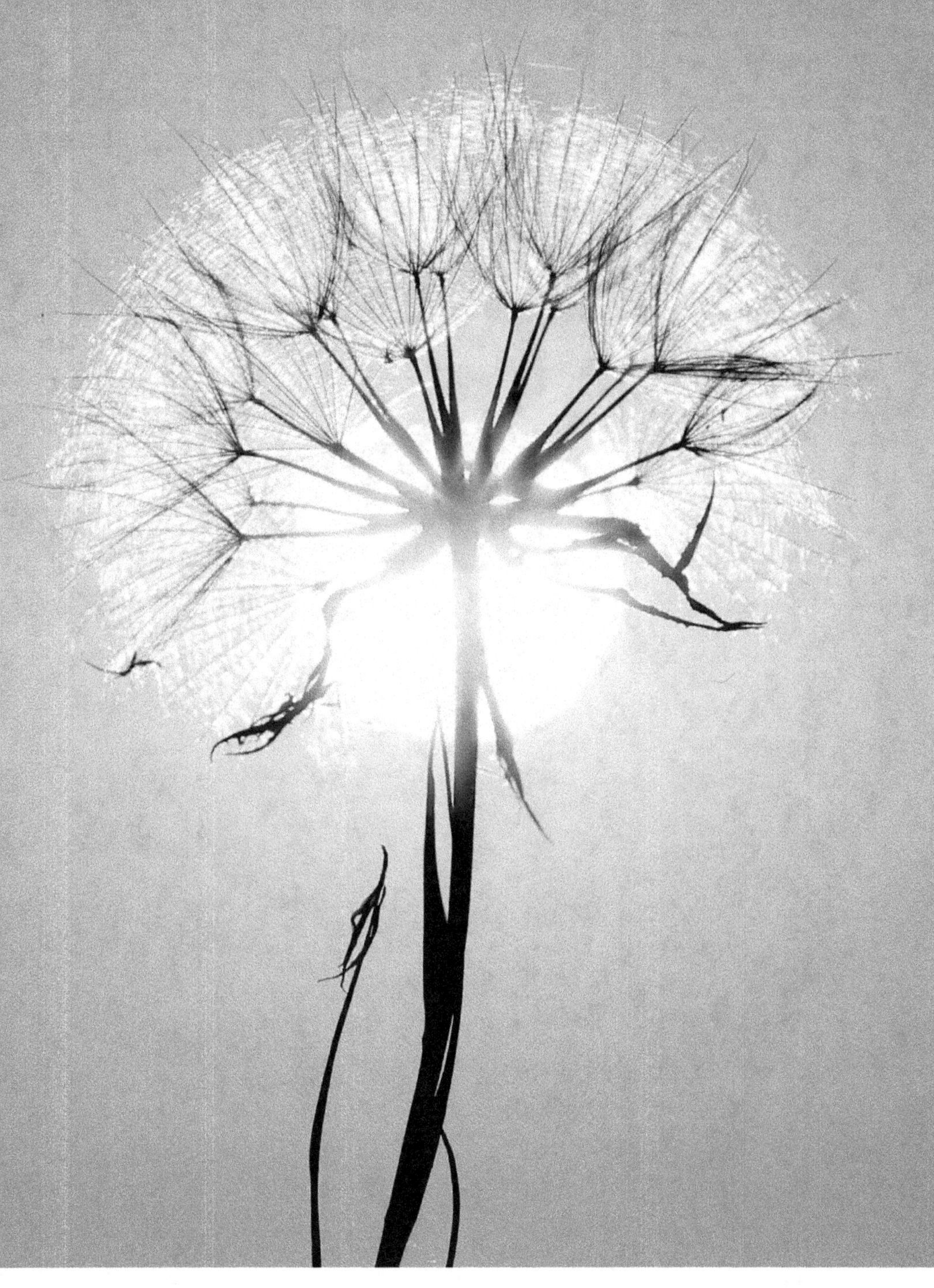

I AM VERY LUCKY TO DO WHAT
I LOVE TO DO AND PROSPER FROM IT.

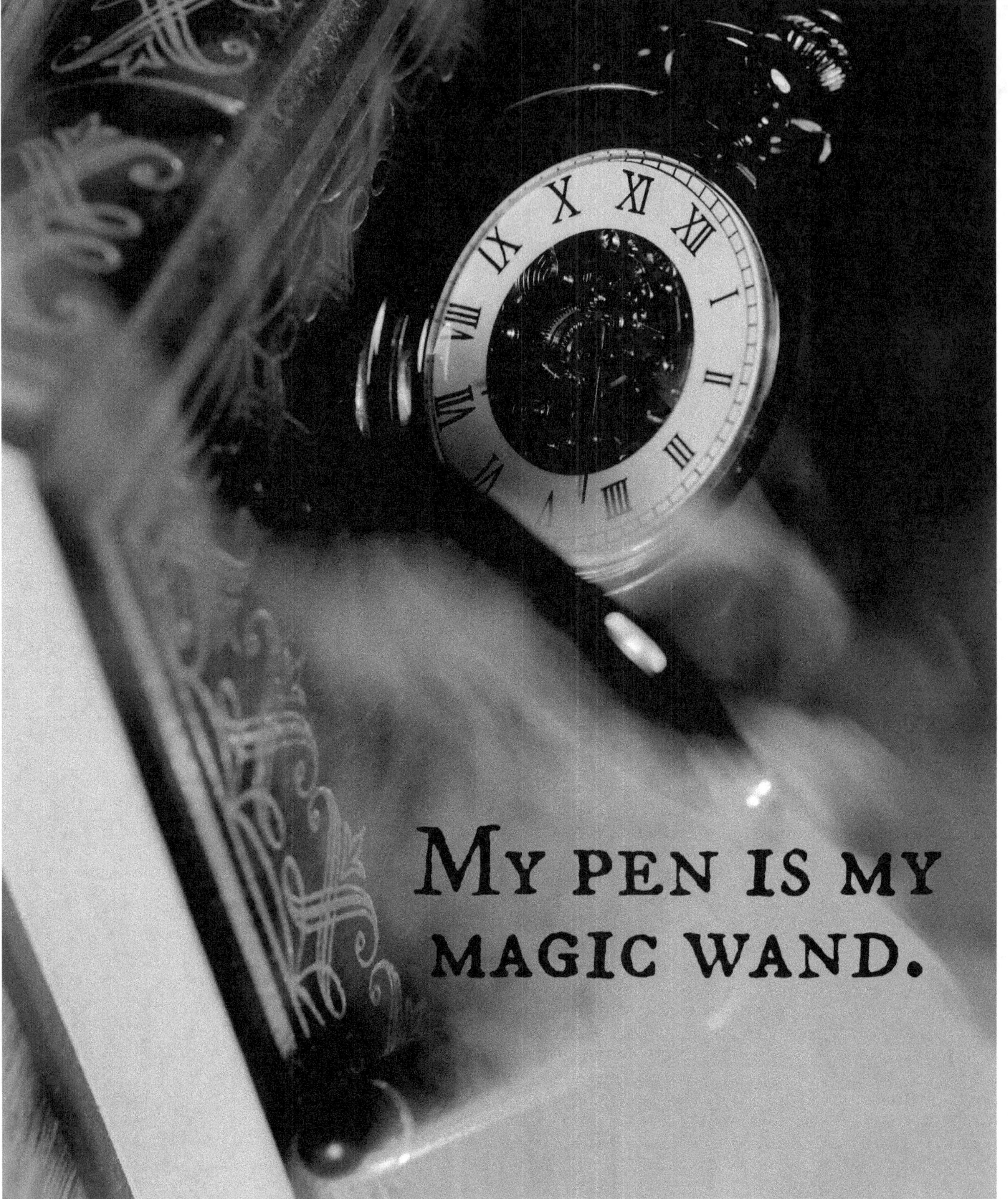
My pen is my magic wand.

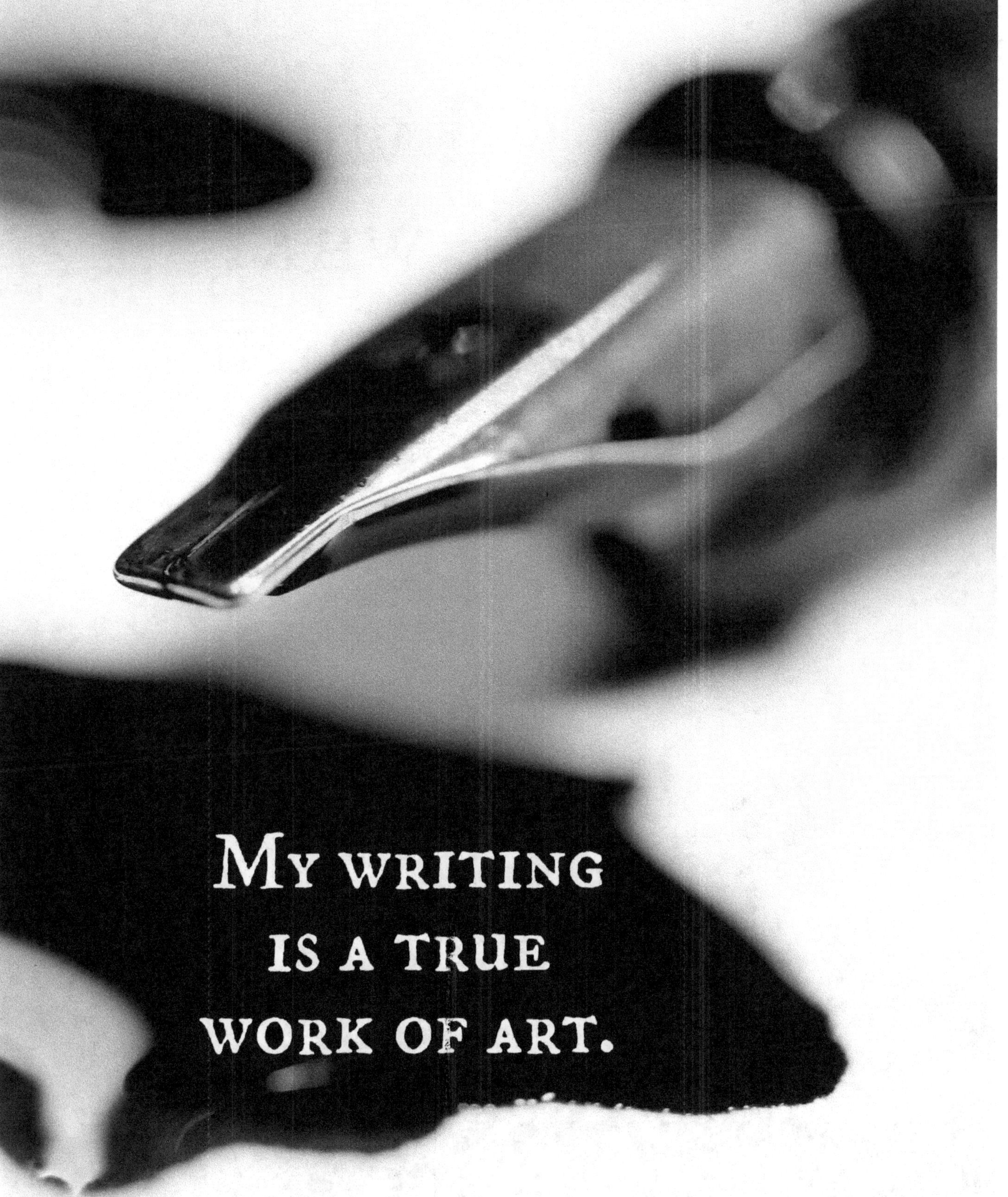
MY WRITING
IS A TRUE
WORK OF ART.

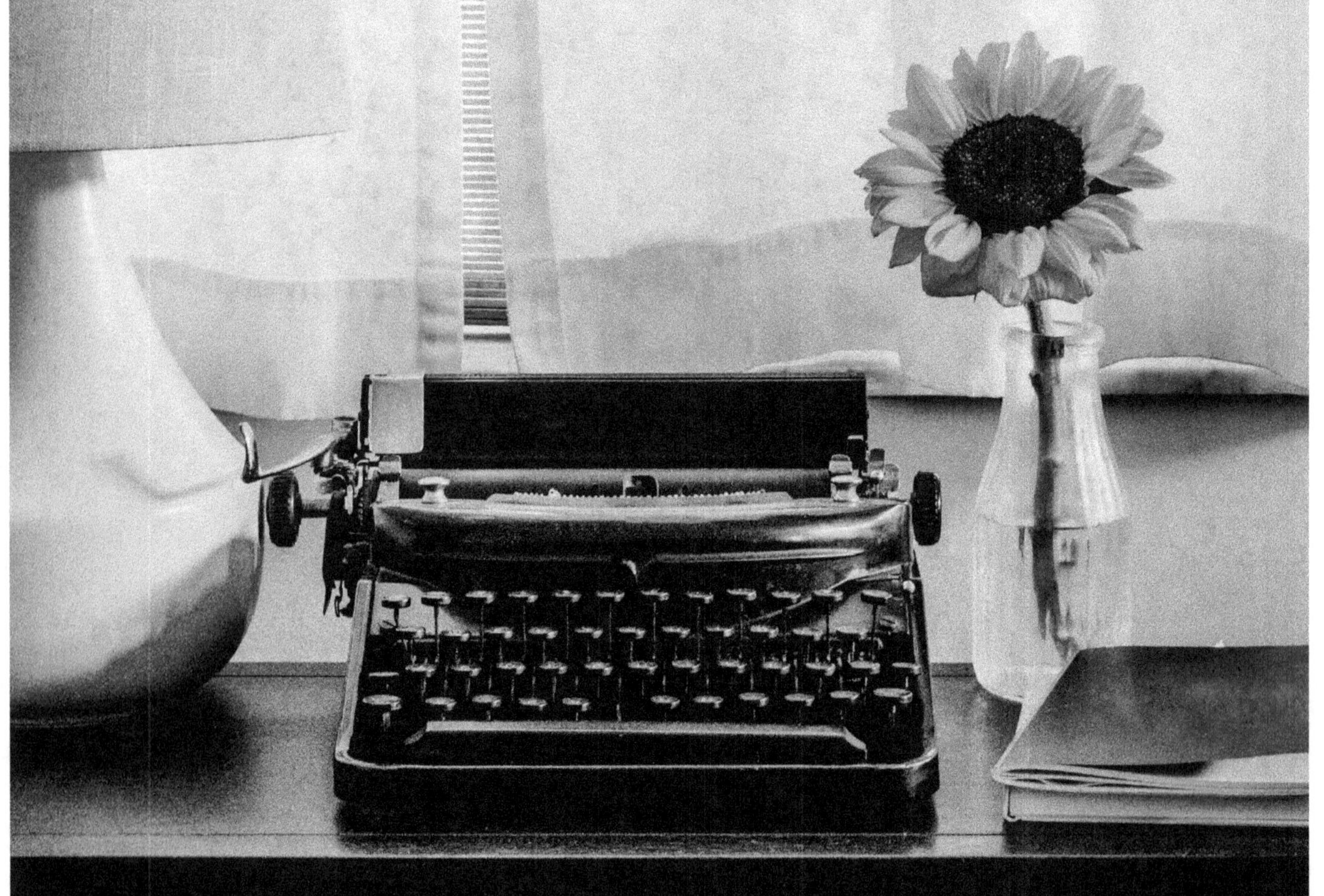

I WRITE
WHAT
I THINK.

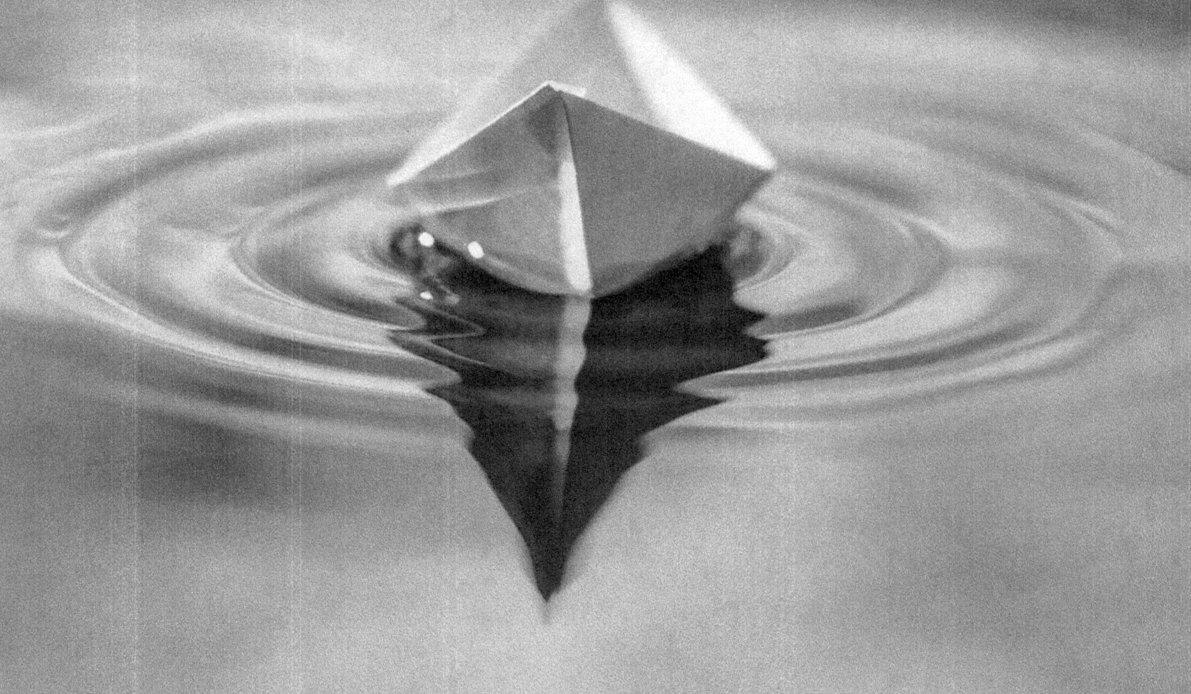
I EXPRESS MY IMAGINATION
FLUENTLY ON PAPER.

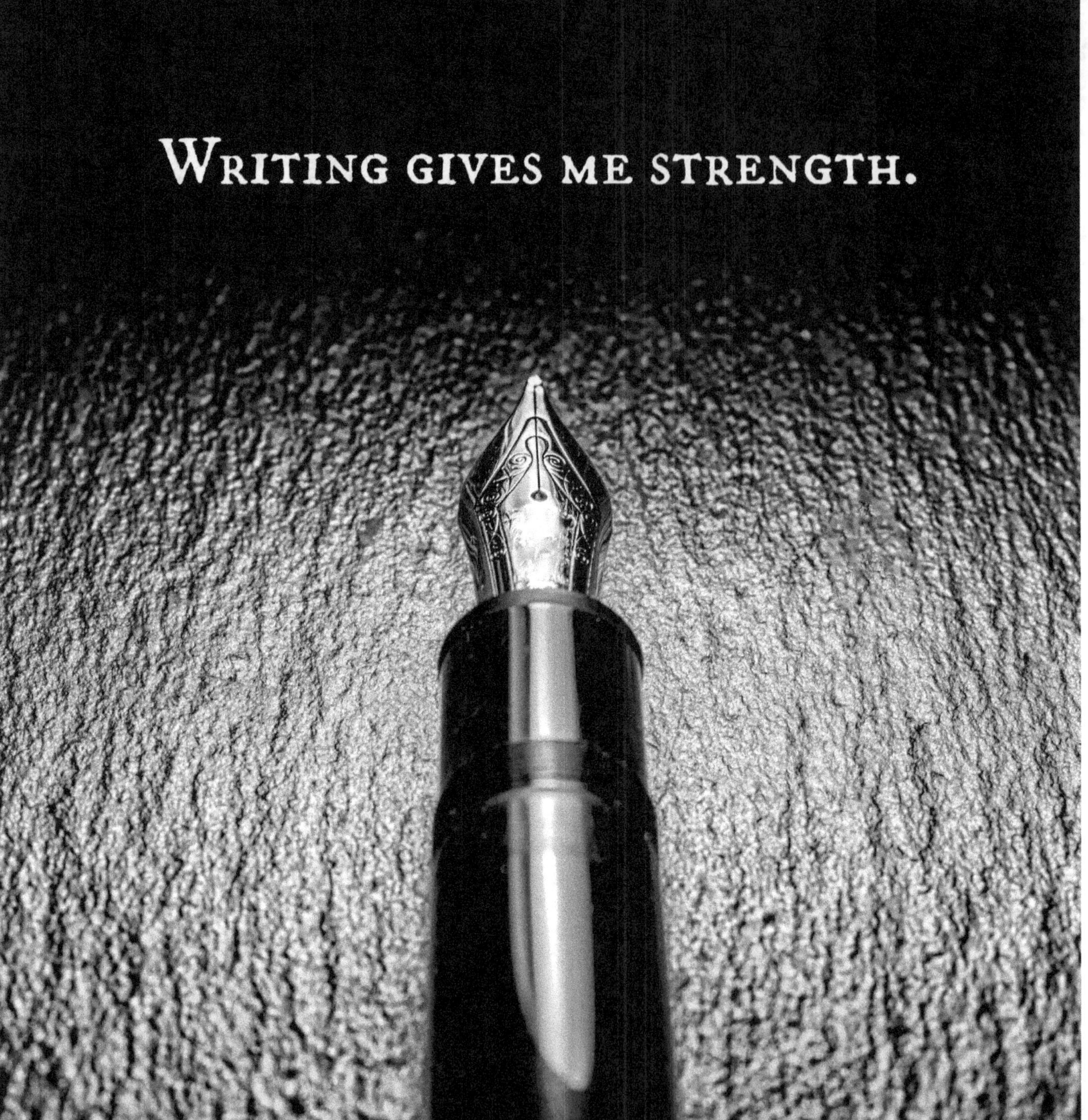
WRITING GIVES ME STRENGTH.

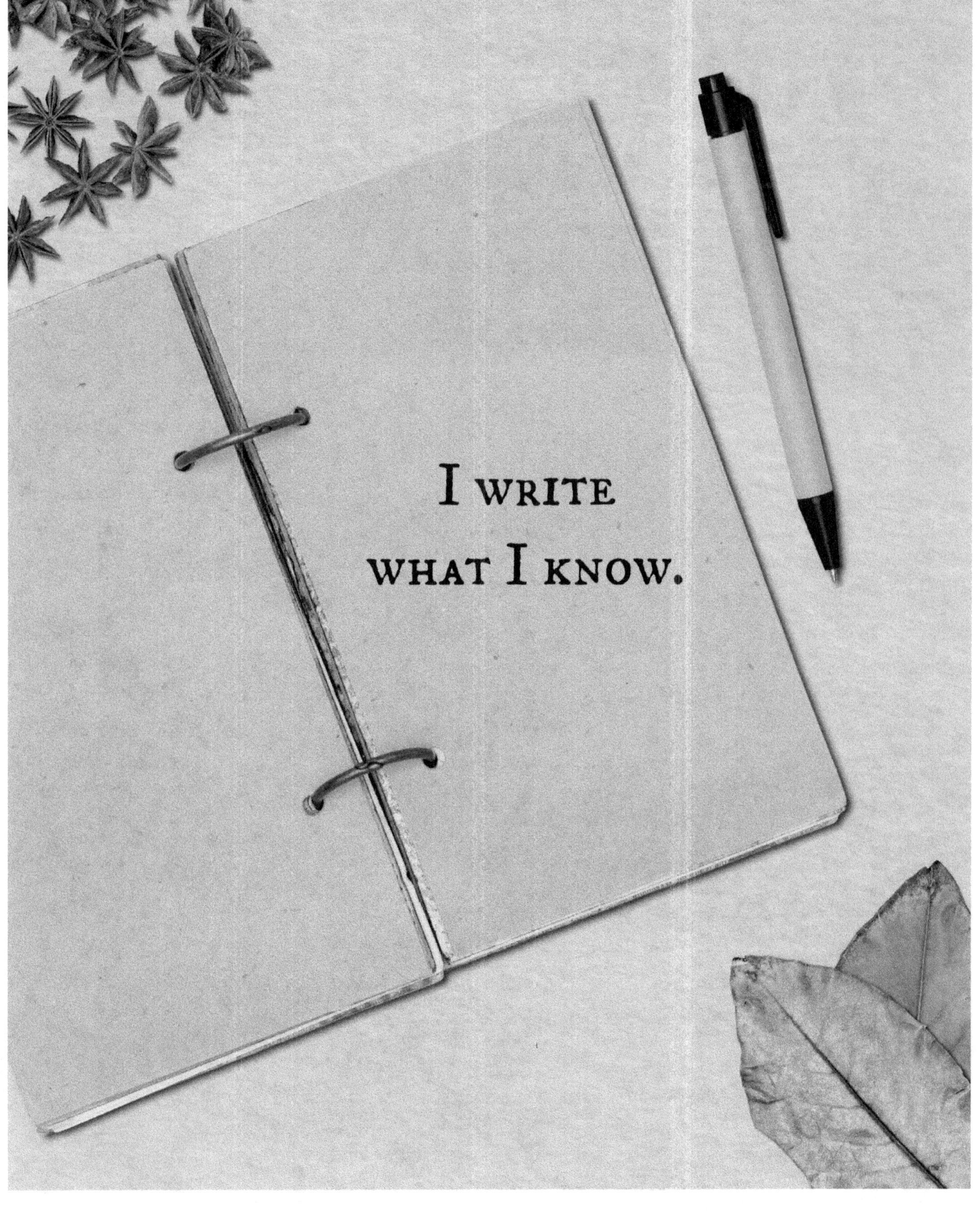

I write
what I know.

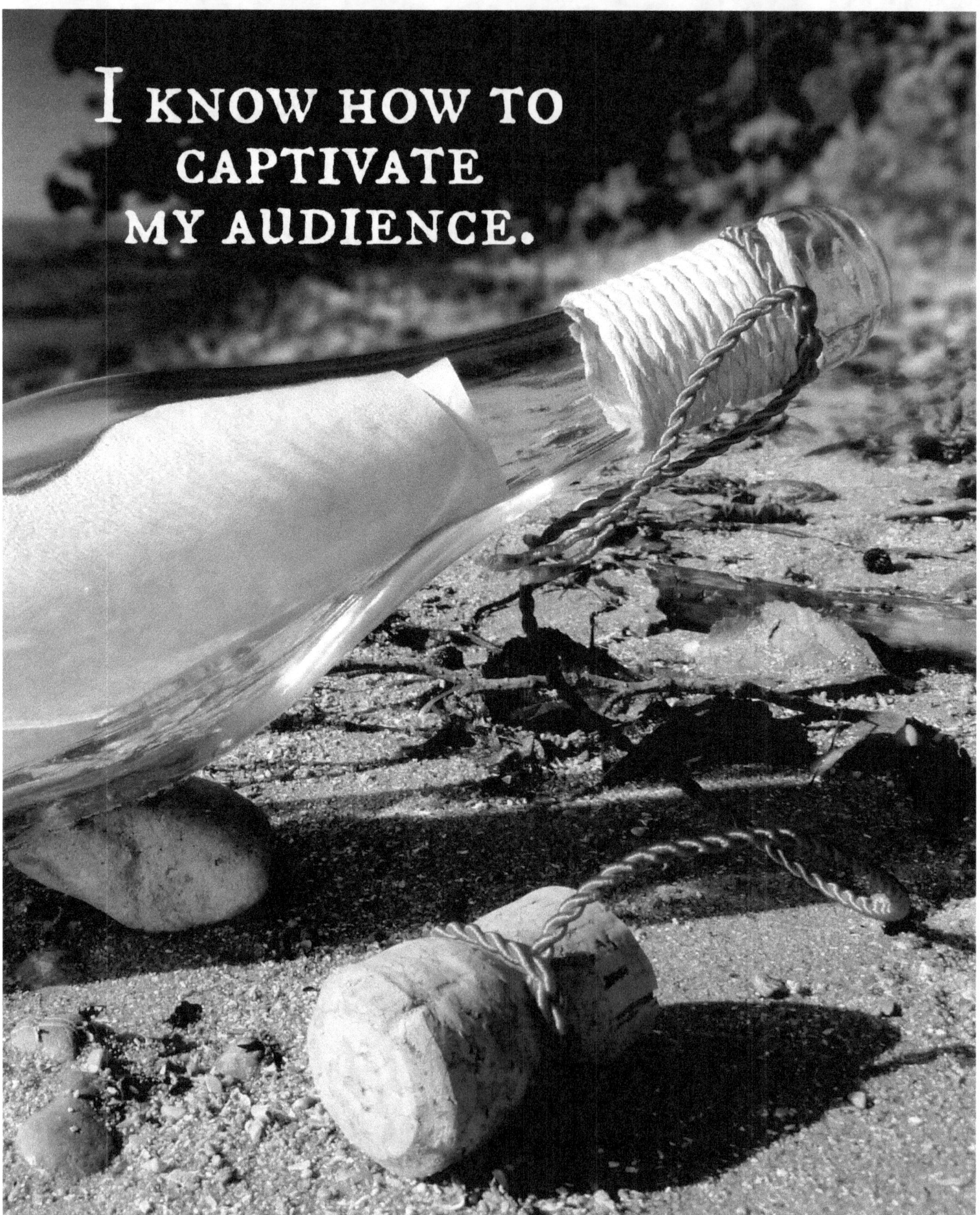
I KNOW HOW TO
CAPTIVATE
MY AUDIENCE.

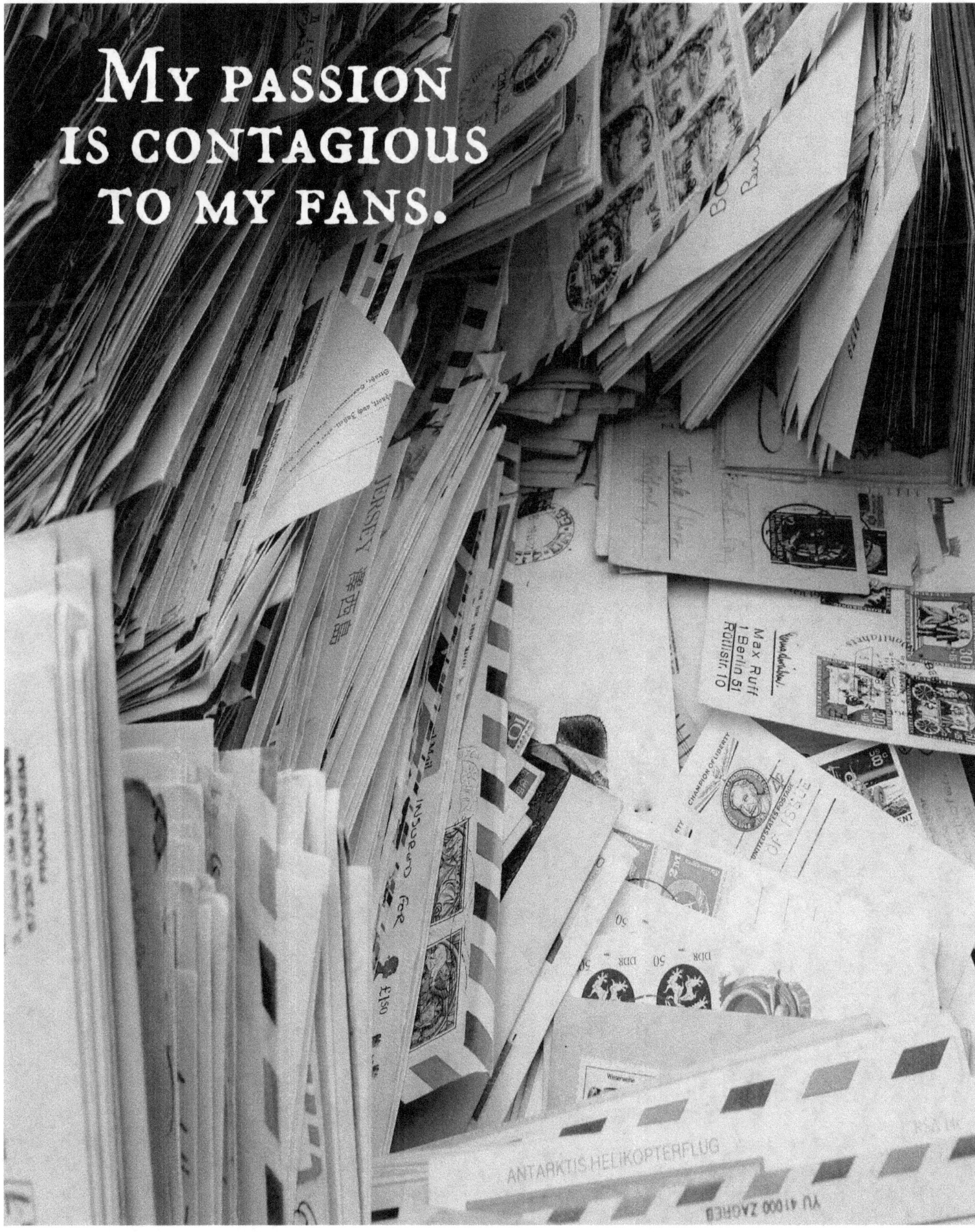
My passion
is contagious
to my fans.

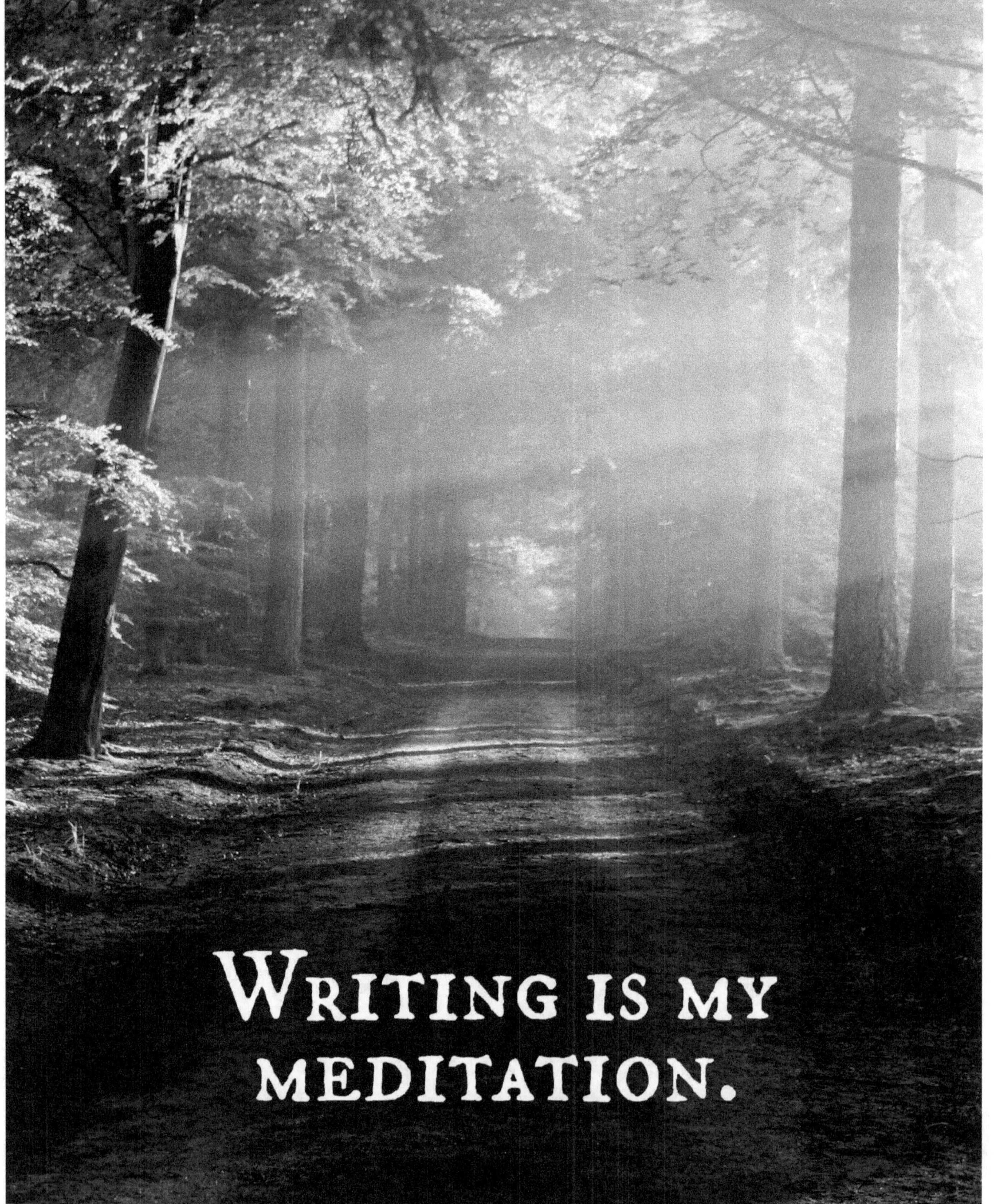
WRITING IS MY
MEDITATION.

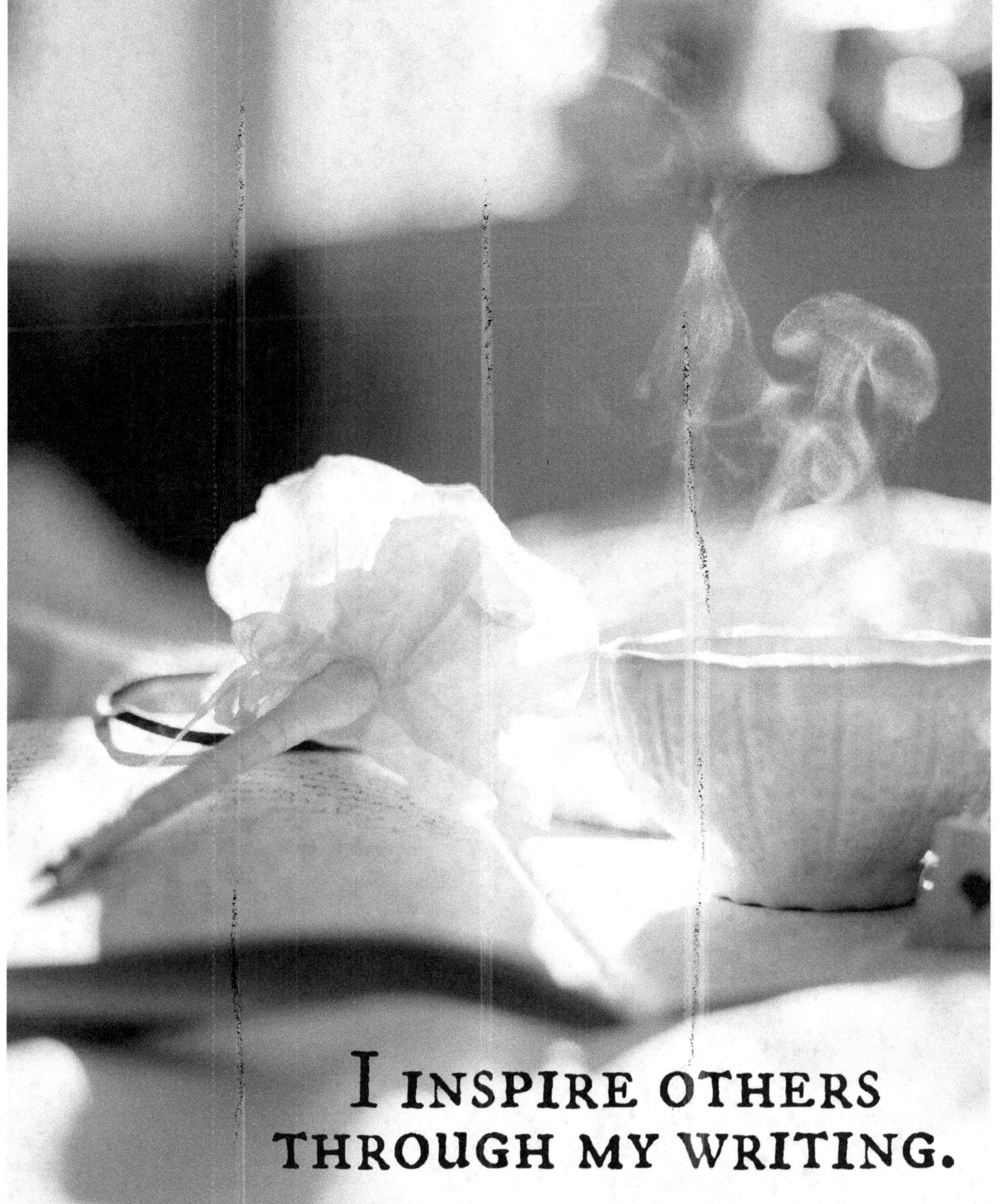
I INSPIRE OTHERS THROUGH MY WRITING.

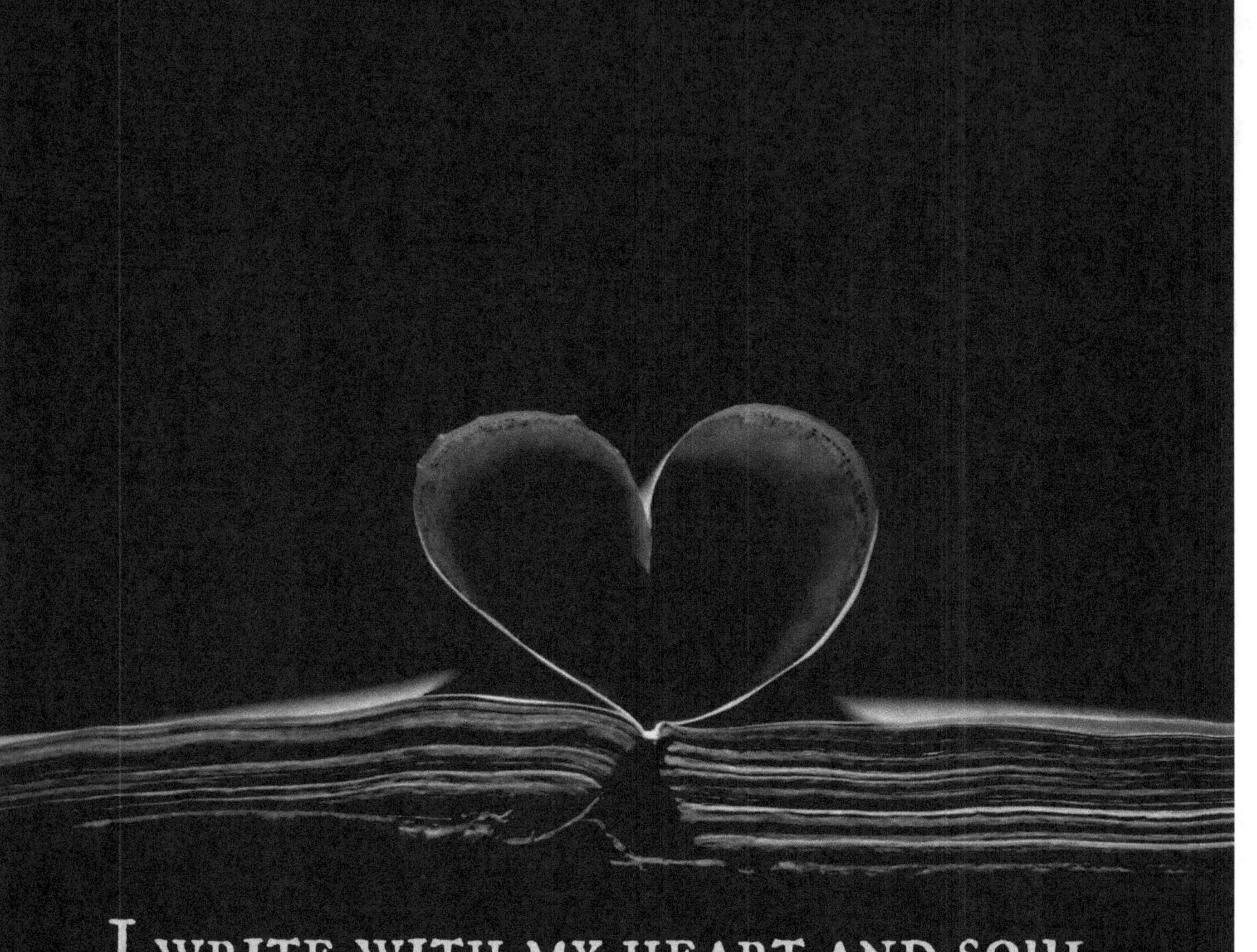

I WRITE WITH MY HEART AND SOUL.

I AM A BEST SELLING AUTHOR.

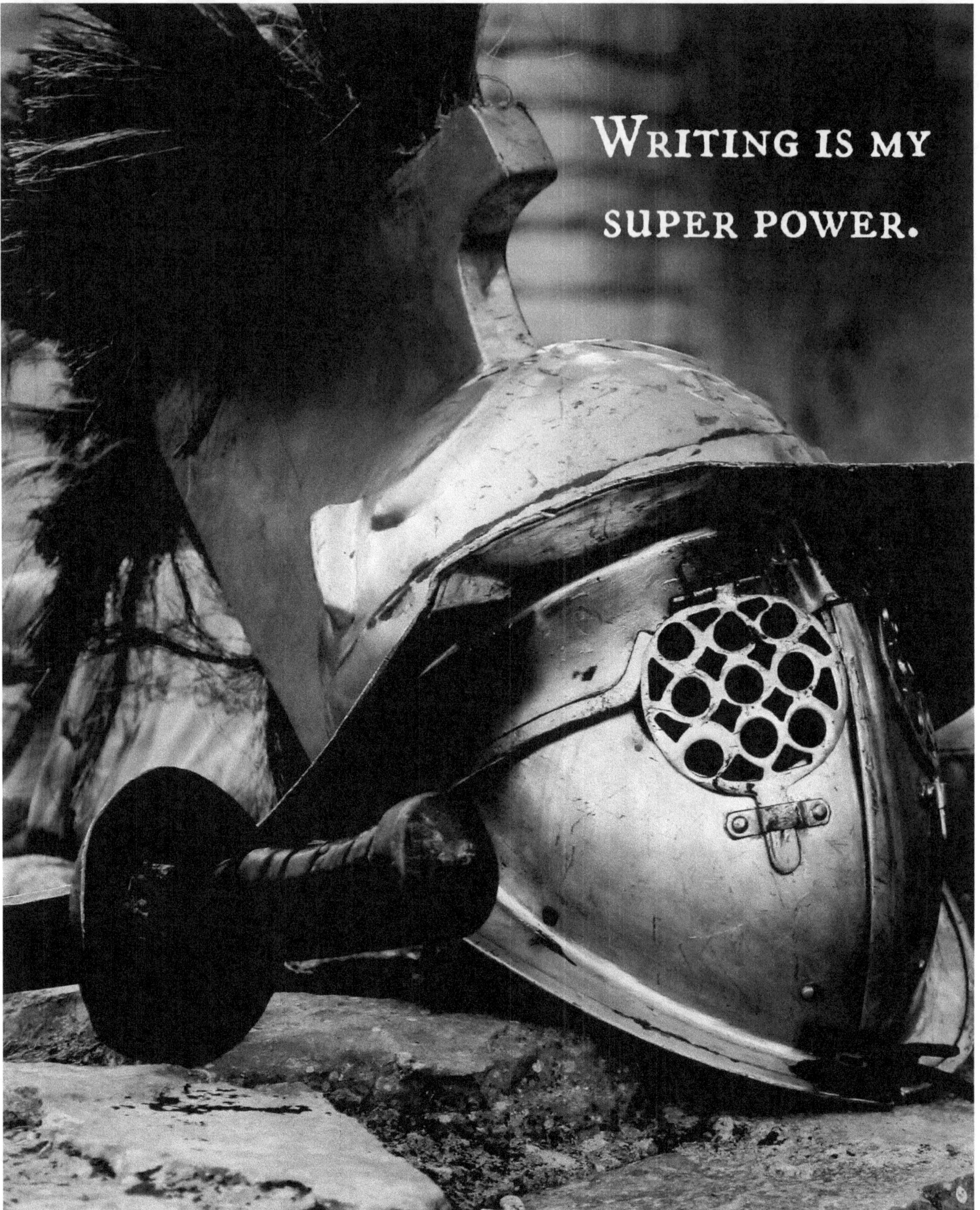
WRITING IS MY
SUPER POWER.

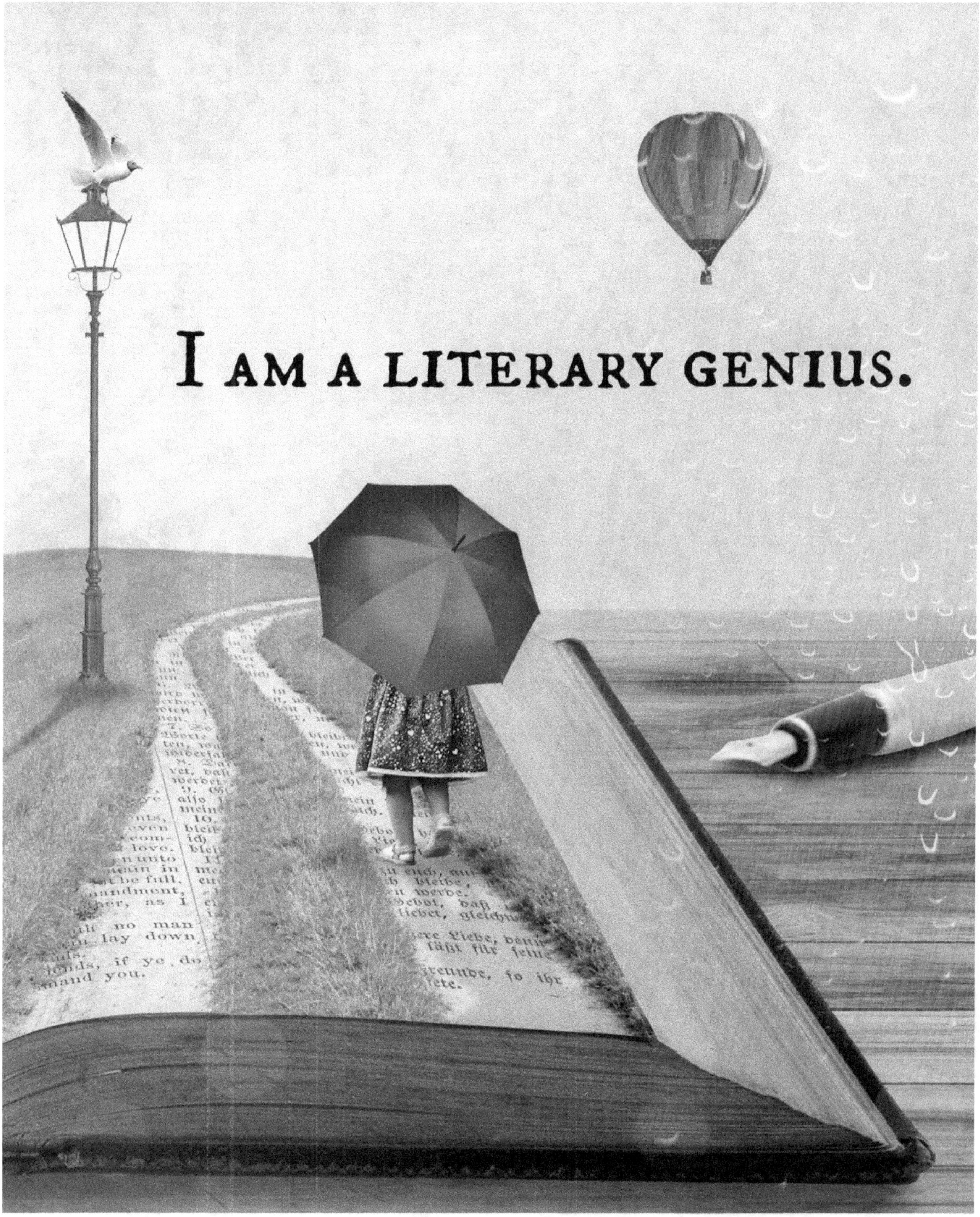

I AM A LITERARY GENIUS.

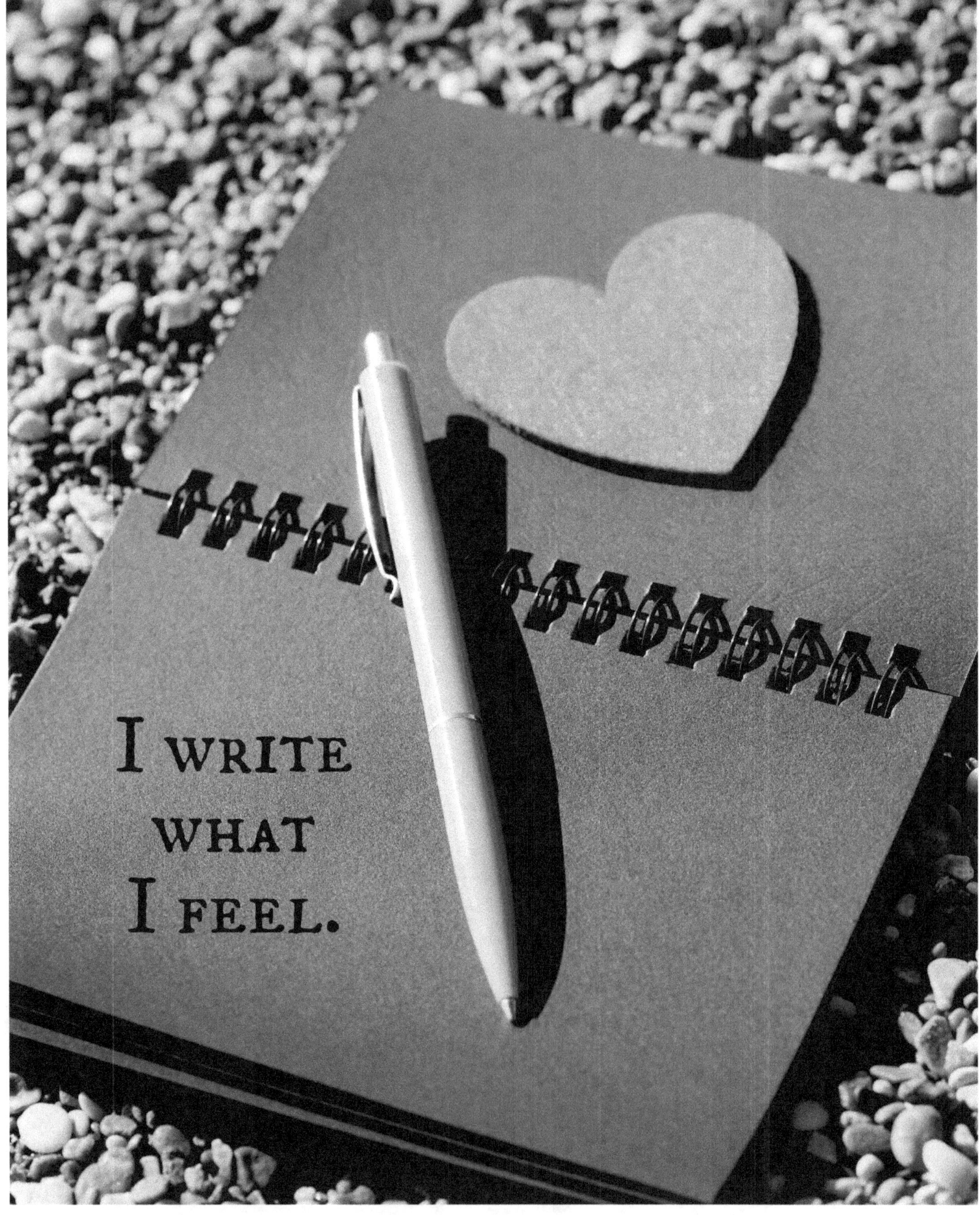
I WRITE
WHAT
I FEEL.

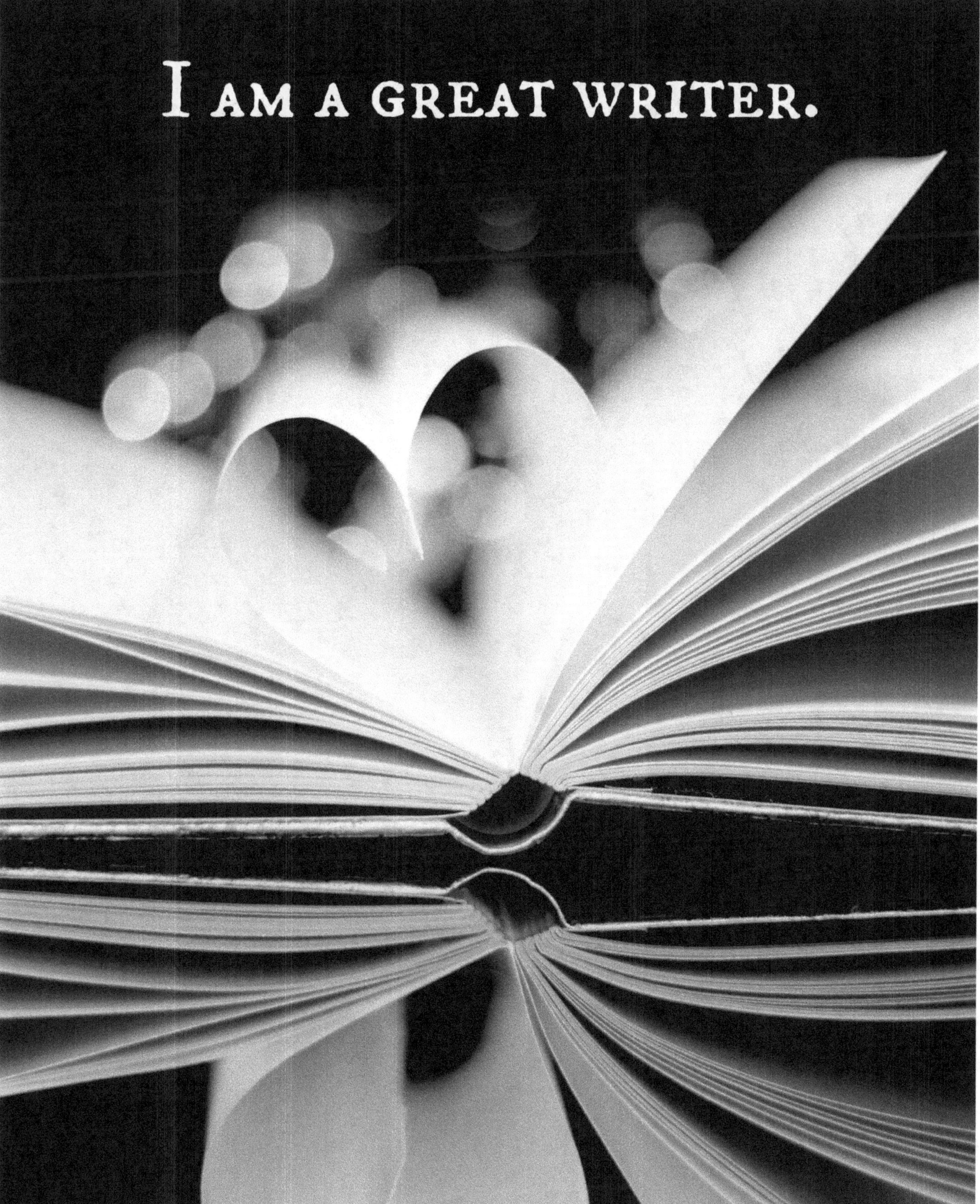
I AM A GREAT WRITER.

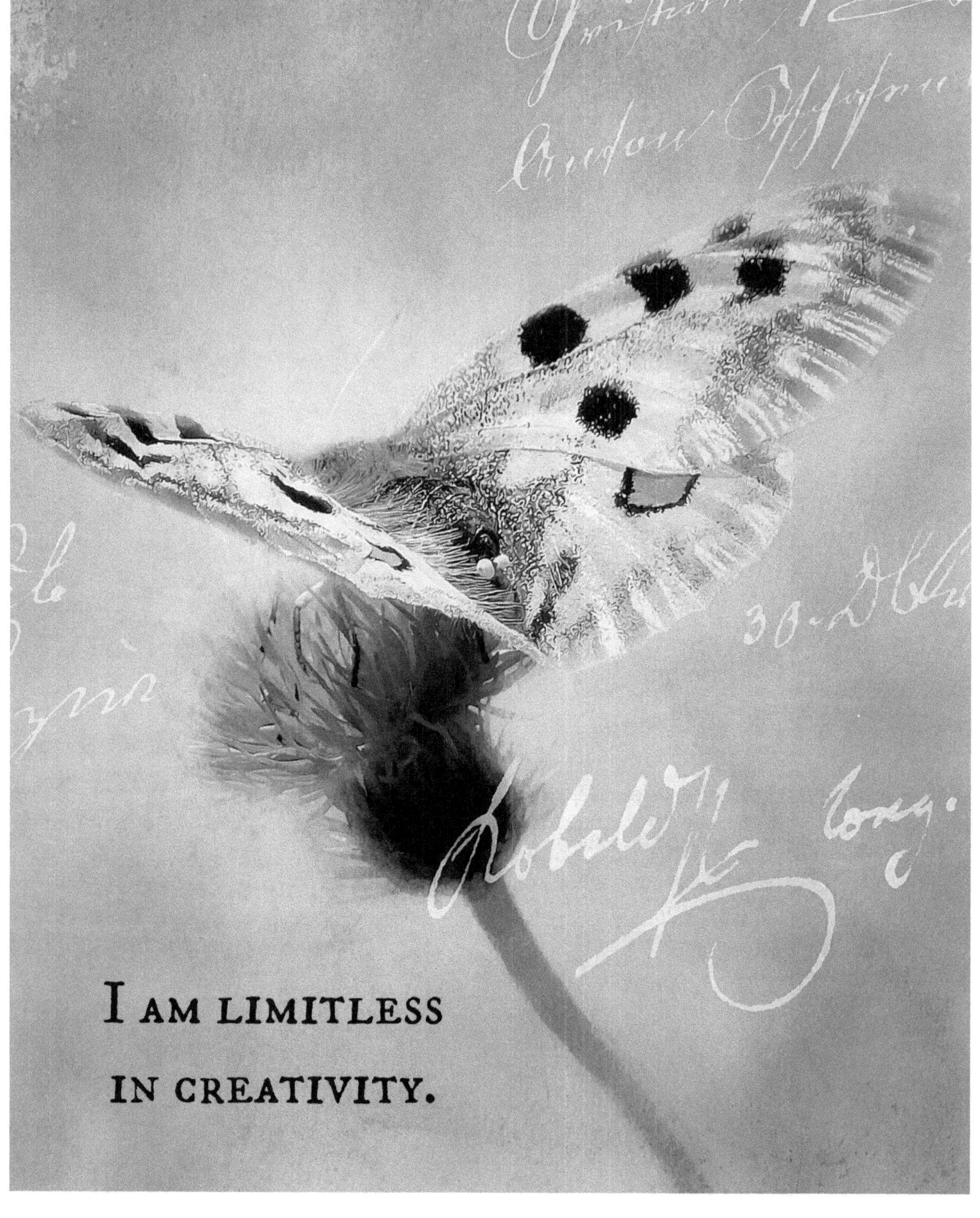

I AM LIMITLESS
IN CREATIVITY.

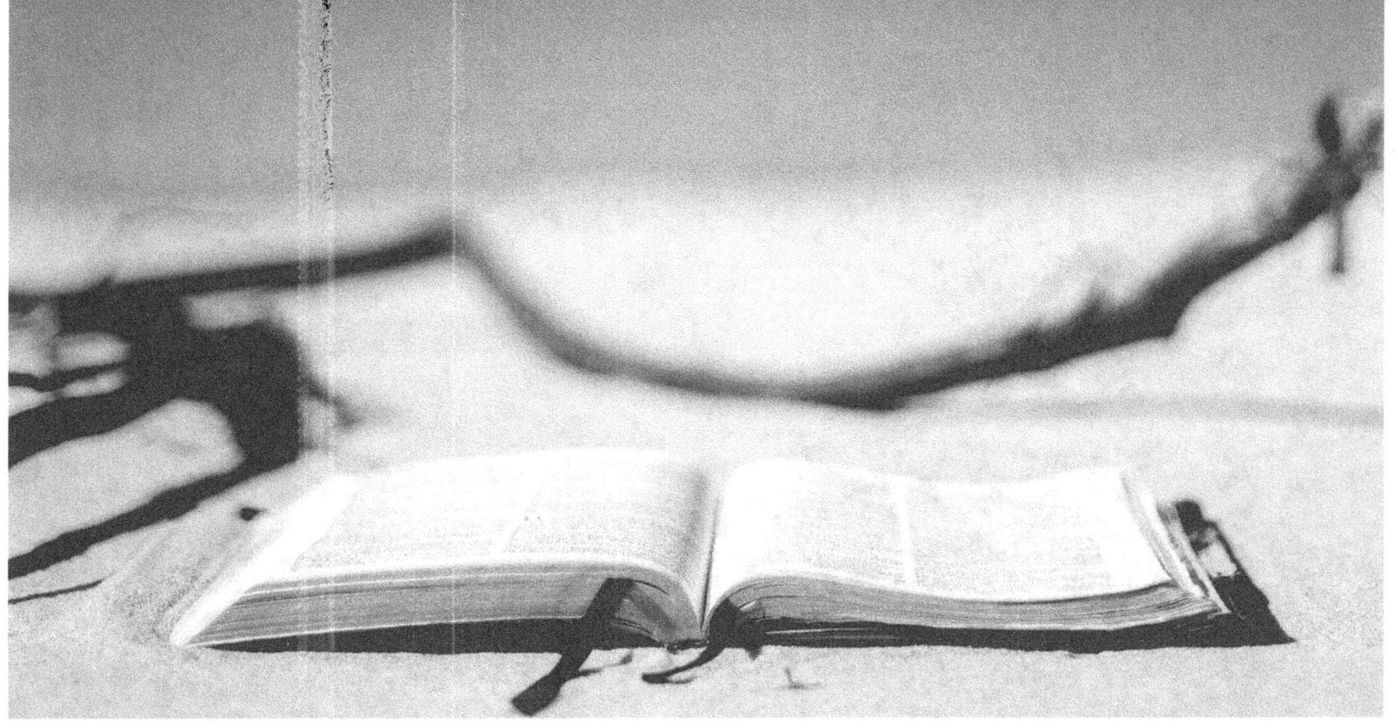

WRITING IS MY DESTINY.

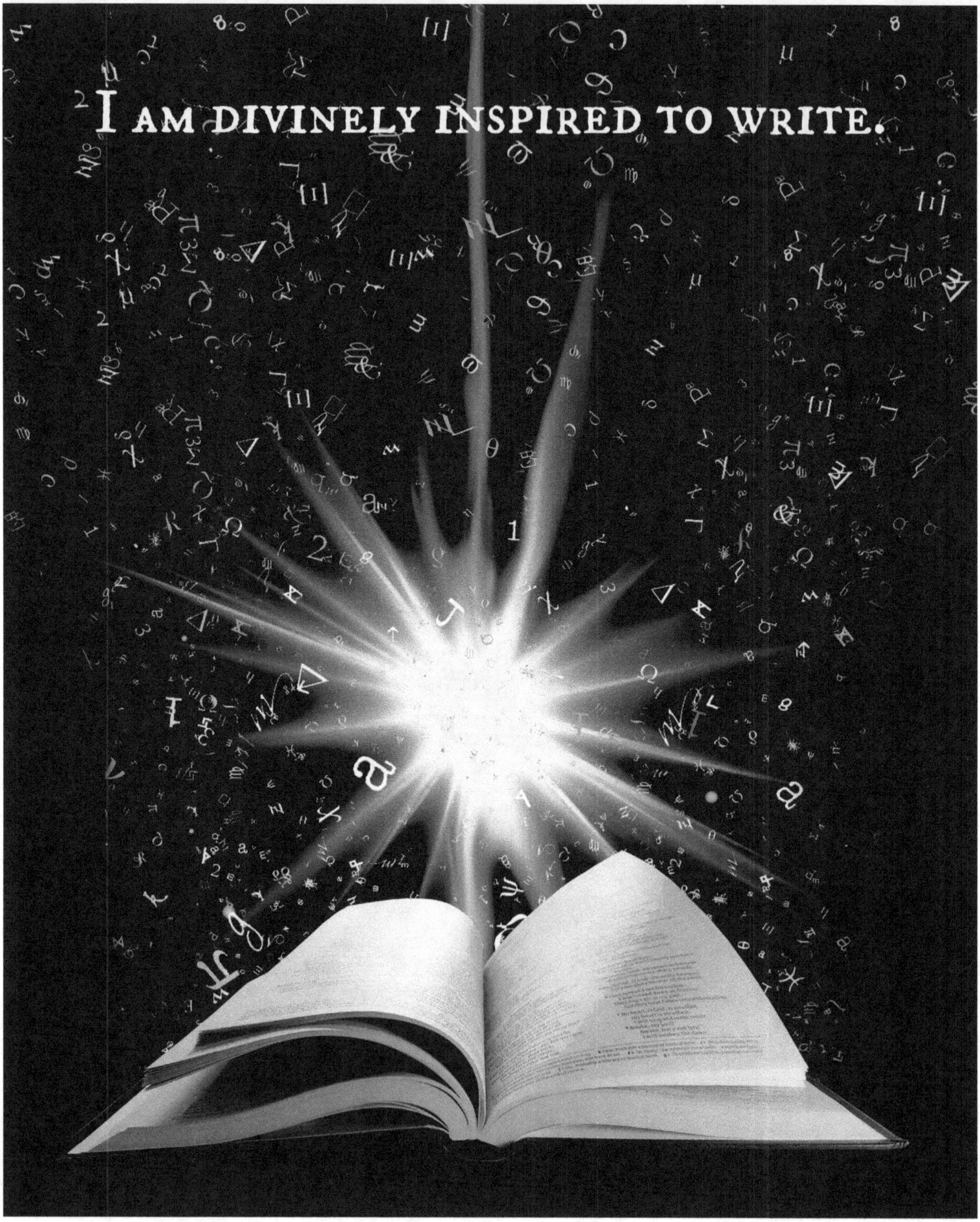

I AM DIVINELY INSPIRED TO WRITE.

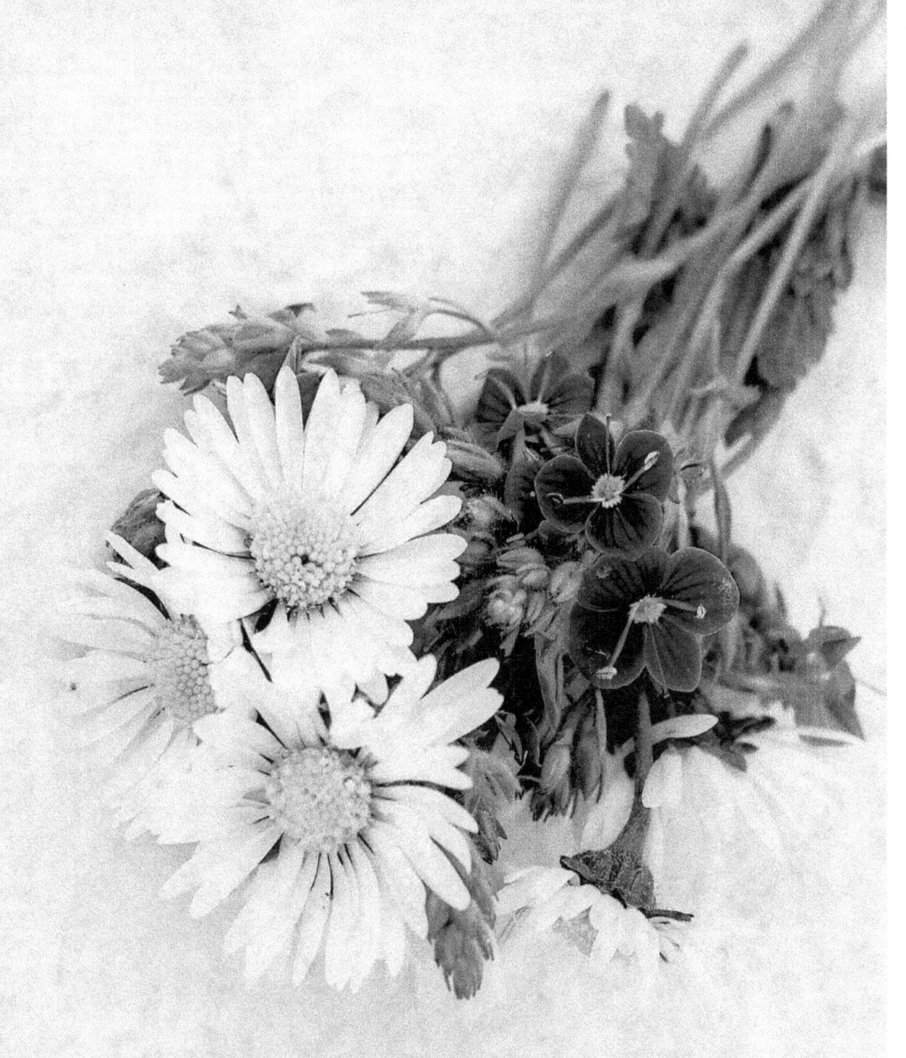

WRITING IS
WHAT I DO BEST.

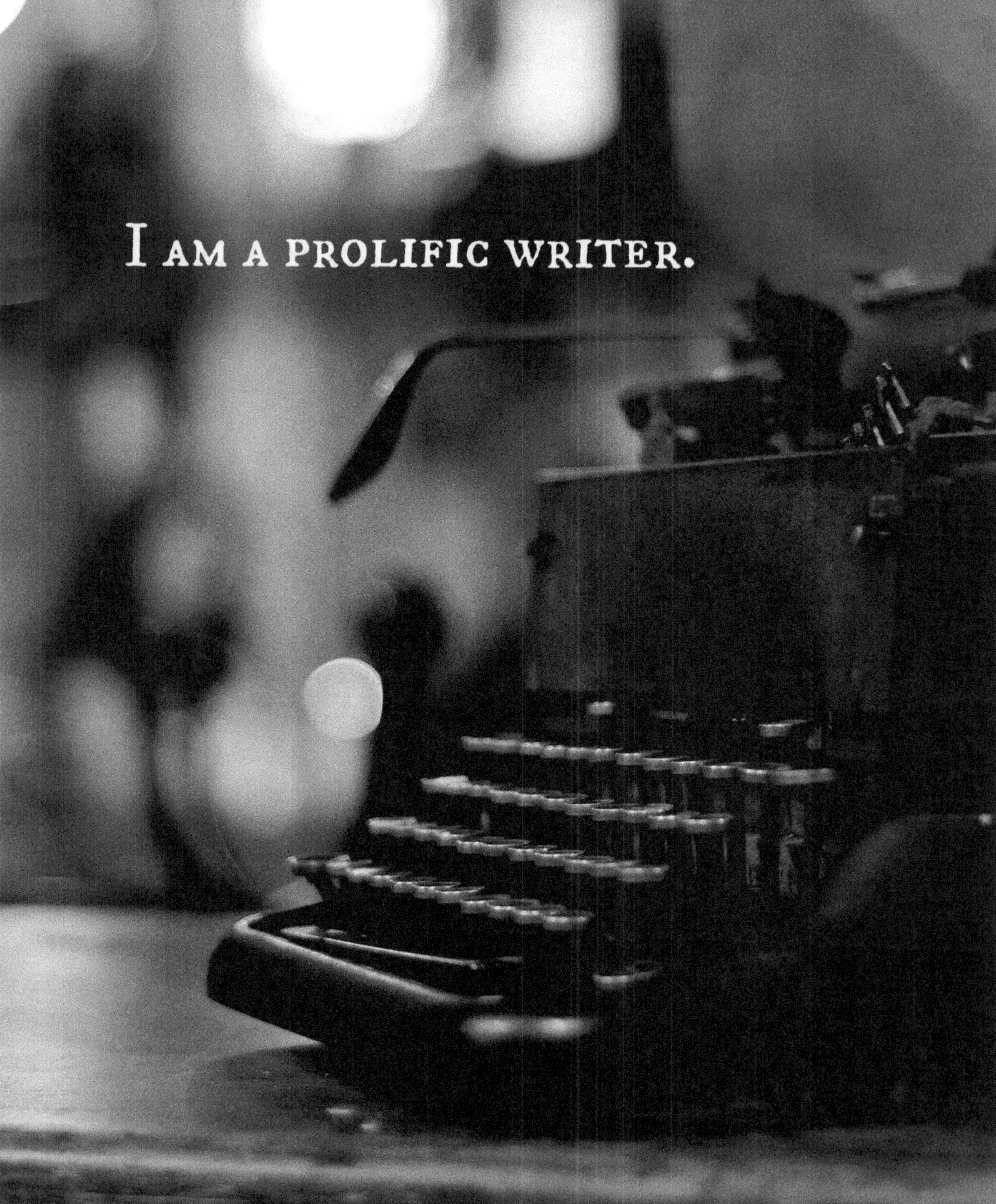
I AM A PROLIFIC WRITER.